URBAN LIFE AND URBAN LANDSCAPE SERIES

Cincinnati in 1840

The Social and Functional Organization of an Urban Community during the Pre-Civil War Period

Walter Stix Glazer

Foreword by Carl Abbott
Afterword by John D. Fairfield

Ohio State University Press

Columbus

Library of Congress Cataloging-in-Publication Data

Glazer, Walter.
    Cincinnati in 1840 : the social and functional organization of an
urban community during the pre–Civil War period / Walter Stix
Glazer; foreword by Carl Abbott, afterword by John D. Fairfield.
        p.   cm. — (Urban life and urban landscape series)
    Originally presented as the author's dissertation (Ph. D.)—
University of Cincinnati, 1974.
    Includes bibliographical references and index.
    ISBN 0-8142-0828-2 (cl : alk. paper). —
ISBN 0-8142-5030-0 (pa : alk. paper).
    1. Cincinnati (Ohio)—History—19th century.   2. Cincinnati
(Ohio)—Social conditions—19th century.   3. Cincinnati—Population—
History—19th century.   4. City and town life—Ohio—Cincinnati—
History—19th century.   I. Title.   II. Series.
F499.C557G53   1999
977.1′7803—dc21   99-22590
                                                                      CIP

Cover design by Paula Newcomb.
Type set in Garamond #3 by Keystone Typesetting, Inc.
Printed by Braun-Brumfield, Inc.

9   8   7   6   5   4   3   2   1

To
SAM HAYS

Contents

Foreword

My first introduction to Walter Glazer's research on the social dynamics of Cincinnati arrived one blustery Chicago afternoon in 1970, packaged in a cheerful yellow and black box from University Microfilms. A few weeks earlier I had been scoping out the competition for a planned dissertation on economic policy making in early midwestern cities. I wanted to look at Chicago because that's where I was studying, Cincinnati because it was close to my family's home in Dayton, and perhaps Indianapolis, for contrast. Jim Madison's work on the Indianapolis business community would be complementary, we eventually concluded. But what about this dissertation on "Cincinnati in 1840" that Walter Glazer had submitted at the University of Michigan in 1968? I needed to break down and order it, I decided.

When I found the time to crank the dissertation through an already rickety Recordak film reader in the University Library, what I found was methodologically sophisticated research that spoke the language of the "new urban history" but posed questions about social institutions and relationships rather than individual life experiences and careers. Indeed, Glazer's theme of growing social pluralism and division has been central to a generation of scholarship on the rise of American cities. Publication of the expanded study, on which Glazer continued to work for several years at the University of Pittsburgh, offers historians the opportunity to see how his analysis resonates with other scholarship in urban history.

The big question structuring "Cincinnati in 1840" is the effects of urban growth on the ideal and practice of community. What happened to Cincinnati's civic values and political culture as a large town (25,000 people in 1830) turned into a city (115,000 people in 1850)? And what happened to its public institutions and social relationships?

This is a venerable question in urban sociology, the root of efforts by small towners such as Robert Park or Jane Addams to understand places like Chicago. It has also been a fertile question for other urban historians of Glazer's generation. Michael Frisch examined similar issues of political and social change in *Town into City: Springfield, Massachusetts and the Meaning of Community, 1840–1880* (1972). Stuart Blumin conveyed the same interest in his title for *The Urban Threshold: Growth and Change in a Nineteenth Century American Community* (1976), as did Roger Lotchin in his subtitle for *San Francisco, 1846–1856: From Hamlet to City* (1974).

This topic of civic culture has attracted attention because the previous generation of urban biographers focused on the formal scaffolding of growth rather than its social consequences. The subject matter for Bessie Pierce, Blake McKelvey, Bayrd Still, and other authors in the 1940s and 1950s was how cities grew: how local government added responsibilities and functions, how railroads were built, how city economies gained industries, how migration added new residents.

Glazer, his contemporaries, and more recent scholars have assumed this framework of development and problematized intra-city relationships and social networks. Glazer asks how growth in the scale of Cincinnati changed the ties and interactions among its residents. Did the big city widen the differences in ideas and expectations between long-term residents and newcomers? Did a tide of European immigrants create the conditions for conflict between native-born and foreign-born? Did the rise of an industrial and corporate economy create conflicts that undermined consensus among workers and the middle classes?

To help answer these questions, Glazer utilized an exciting new "intellectual technology." As did many of us, he mined city directories and manuscript census returns for information on individual Cincinnatians, dropped off rubber-banded stacks of punched cards at the university mainframe, and pored over the resulting fan-folded printouts. Unlike a number of scholars who trained their sights on the question of individual mobility and opportunity, however, Glazer treated his Cincinnatians not as atomized individuals but as members of a complexly structured society. His pyramidal model of Cincinnati society combines multiple views of social class that draw on a Marxian interest in economic stratification and Weberian ideas of class as ascribed position (old timer versus newcomer, in the Cincinnati version).

Within this broad framework, Glazer engaged several specific issues that continue to be the subjects of lively scholarly debate. His examination of community values adds to debates over urban boosterism. *Cincinnati in 1840* supports those historians who see urban boosterism as a widely shared community vision with the ability to mobilize large segments of the population around a public agenda. Examples include Gunther Barth, *Instant Cities: Urbanization and the Rise of San Francisco and Denver* (1975), David Hamer, *New Towns in the New World: Images and Perceptions of the Nineteenth-Century Frontier* (1990), and my own *Boosters and Businessmen: Economic Thought and Urban Growth in the Antebellum Middle West* (1981). In contrast, Glazer's work gives less support to those who see boosterism as an ideology that business leaders imposed on fragmented communities, a point argued by Robert Dykstra in *The Cattle Towns* (1968) and by Don Doyle in *The Social Order of a Frontier Community: Jacksonville, Illinois, 1825–1870* (1978).

Glazer's work also expands our understanding of the processes of ethnic group formation and isolation. Like Kathleen Conzen in *Immigrant Milwaukee, 1836–1860: Accommodation and Community in a Frontier City* (1976) and David Gerber in *The Making of an American Pluralism: Buffalo, New York, 1825–1860* (1989), Glazer sees the large German immigration of the 1840s and 1850s as crucial to this process. Growing numbers allowed Germans in Cincinnati to support parochial community institutions as an alternative to participating in the civic arena defined by the old elite.

In turn, ethnic separation was one of the sources of the increasing class polarization. Steven Ross has described the growth of labor-management conflict in *Workers on the Edge: Work, Leisure, and Politics in Industrializing Cincinnati, 1788–1890* (1985). Glazer's interpretation differs from Ross's because of differing definitions of class—whether the trajectory of the Cincinnati elite is best understood as merchants becoming industrialists (Ross), or as old timers becoming marginalized with generational and ethnic change (Glazer).

The portrait of associational life in early Cincinnati highlights the importance of voluntary organizations in American life. This is scarcely a new insight, since it lies at the center of Alexis de Tocqueville's analysis of the American polity—Glazer's own starting point—but the "third sector" was long treated as an ancillary of formal government. In the 1990s, however, the role of the voluntary sector has become a lively field of study with its own organization, the Association for Research on Nonprofit Organizations and Voluntary Action. Historians such as David Hammack, Peter Dobkin Hall, and Thomas Bender have been active contributors to the field.

Finally, Glazer's exploration of political values and their practical expressions contributes to our understanding of changing conceptions of the civic realm during the nineteenth century. Many historians now posit that an ideal of republicanism animated public life in the nation's first two generations. Marked by a willingness to pursue self-interest within a larger commitment to community, republicanism was presumably eroded and corroded by liberal individualism through the course of the nineteenth century.

Cincinnati in 1840 uses different terminology to offer a case study of this process. Glazer describes a shift during the 1840s from voluntary associations to political parties as the avenues for civic action. "Because voluntary associations usually were not competing with one another, in purpose or for members," he writes, "they were more compatible and engendered a more corporate concept of society. Because political parties were in direct conflict with one another, over principles and popular support, they were more divisive and encouraged a more fragmented concept of society."

Glazer's study thus identifies a pivotal era. Had he focused on twenty years earlier, as did Daniel Aaron in *Cincinnati, Queen City of the West: 1819–1838* (1992), he would have found a basically unified public culture. Had he started with the 1850s and 1860s, he would have found a polity that increasingly revolved around conflict by ethnicity, race, class, and industrial interest. By splitting the difference, he describes a pivotal era in a city whose history poses questions that are still central to the problem of civic action.

CARL ABBOTT

Preface

Thirty-three years ago—in the summer of 1966—I started research on Cincinnati during the pre–Civil War period in order to complete my Ph.D. in history at the University of Michigan. My intention was to focus on the period between 1840 and 1860, when the city experienced its most dramatic growth and was transformed by immigration and industrialization. More broadly, I hoped to use my analysis as a case study of Jacksonian democracy: an examination of how the radical individualism and mobility that Tocqueville described in *Democracy in America* actually worked within a large and dynamic urban community.

As I delved into the newspapers, I was struck by the number and variety of lists of names of people who were involved in a variety of local activities. Who were these people? Gradually, I collected these lists from the various sources for 1840, transferred the names to index cards, and recorded personal information about the people from the city directory, tax lists, and the 1840 census. In the fall I put this information onto IBM punchcards and conducted the tedious process of running them through a card sorter to profile these people and their various activities for a paper, "Participation and Power: A Social Analysis of Voluntary Associations in Cincinnati in 1840."

That winter Sam Hays offered me a position teaching urban history at the University of Pittsburgh. He said he liked what I was doing and encouraged me to do a more systematic and comprehensive study of Cincinnati during the pre–Civil War period. Over the next six years I completed the dissertation and expanded it into a manuscript that was accepted for publication in 1974. The following year, I had a sabbatical and went to New Zealand as Visiting Fulbright Professor at the University of Auckland, and soon decided to remain as a permanent resident. One of the consequences was that the Cincinnati manuscript was never published.

After the manuscript had sat gathering dust for more than twenty years, Zane Miller called me to ask whether I would consider submitting it to him for possible publication. By this time I had made the transition from academia to market research and management consulting and had completely lost touch with the field of American urban history.

I talked to several people to get their opinion on the manuscript and its current value. They informed me that urban historians are no longer interested in the issue of social structure and mobility and that quantitative research has gone out of fashion. However, they also said that the manuscript deals with some issues that are now becoming more interesting to urban historians and sociologists (such as the prevalence and role of voluntary associations in American history) and that no one else has used this kind of analysis and model to describe urban communities. Based on this feedback, I agreed to submit the manuscript for publication with the understanding that it would stand as written in 1974 (with minor editorial changes). Carl Abbott has generously agreed to write a foreword that places my work in a broader historiographical and contemporary context.

In reviewing the manuscript, I can recall at least some of what I was trying to do and, at the same time, look at the work with the perspective of more than two decades of time and experience. As I have tried to suggest, the study began with a rather vague focus on Cincinnati during the pre–Civil War period and an interest in Jacksonian society (as described by Tocqueville), but it soon became driven largely by my growing interest in the sources of information about the people living in the city (newspaper lists, city directories, census records, tax lists, etc.).

The challenge was to try to understand these data, and how to use them to describe Cincinnati in 1840 and, more broadly, Jacksonian urban society. I read widely in the literature in urban history and sociology and got some useful conceptual and methodological ideas, but nothing seemed to provide the kind of example, or model, I needed for my work.

As my study expanded from its initial focus on voluntary associational activity to the demographic and social composition of the population, to the role of booster ideology, geographical stability, and economic opportunity as cohesive forces in the community, a picture of the social and functional organization of the Cincinnati community gradually developed in my mind, which I eventually came to think of in terms of a dynamic conical model.

Several historiographical points are worth noting here. I was working during the late 1960s–early 1970s, when the "new urban history," which focused on geographical and socioeconomic mobility, was very popular. I knew this literature, and many of the proponents of this approach, but never felt part of it. I found it too frustrating methodologically and limited conceptually: since most people "disappeared" over time, it was impossible for historians to determine what happened to them or why.

In many respects, I was more influenced by community studies done by colonial historians, who used rich archival records to describe in great detail the social organization and evolution of small New England towns. The focus in this work was more on cohesion, control, and continuity (or breakdown) of communities. I was also encouraged by Merle Curti's pioneering but now-forgotten attempt, in *The Making of An American Community,* to quantitatively document the development of frontier democracy in nineteenth-century Wisconsin, according to the Turner thesis.

As a conceptual and methodological framework, Eric Lampard's essays outlining the relationship between population, economy, social organization, civic leadership, and civic culture in the historical analysis of urbanization were enormously challenging. They led me to sociological literature, particularly the classic and more contemporary community studies. Sociologists provided conceptual and methodological direction that I found quite relevant to the things I was working with in Cincinnati.

And last, but hardly least, Daniel Aaron's "Cincinnati, 1818–1838: A Study of Attitudes in the Urban West" was an inspiration. I read this monumental dissertation, written in 1942, during my first summer of research at the Cincinnati Historical Society and was overwhelmed by Aaron's description of the local society, which was based not only on traditional sources but also on detailed biographical information about the people (including an appendix listing the leading citizens and their organizational affiliations on a large graph-paper matrix).

But why should anyone read this book today? At this stage in my life, I have completely lost touch with the academic literature on Jacksonian America, but I see references to Tocqueville in the press and on television suggesting that people are still interested in the questions about democracy and the role of voluntary associations I raised in my study. I have also been told, by several people who should know, that there is still no good historical study of Cincinnati between 1830 and 1860; this is unfortunate because this is the period of the city's most dynamic growth and change, which must be understood in order to fully appreciate its subsequent history. This void in the literature is also unfortunate because Cincinnati was representative, in many respects, of American urbanization before the Civil War, and despite the large number of monographs on this period, there are still a number of important questions to be answered about the character and composition of urban society at this time.

If these assumptions are valid (and I assume the people who read this will probably be able to judge for themselves), what can my study contribute that is new, important, and useful? The following paragraphs attempt to summarize, from my current perspective, what I believe to be its most relevant contributions.

In the opening chapter on ideology, I tried to show how the combination of rapid growth and aggressive boosterism created a spirit of boundless optimism in Cincinnati that not only defined the special history and character of the community but also stimulated its future development. Obviously, not everyone shared in this experience and vision in 1840, but I still think this booster spirit had a strong and cohesive influence on the community. Later, particularly after 1850, as the rate of population growth slowed down, this sense of confidence and uniqueness declined. I believe this booster spirit is important not only in understanding the unique dynamism of pre–Civil War Cincinnati but also the prevailing optimism of Jacksonian America and boomtowns throughout our history.

In the second chapter on demography, I tried to articulate the composition of the adult white male population of Cincinnati based on data from the 1840 census and city directory. I was aware then (and have been reminded since) that I omitted the majority of the population at this time: women, children, and African Americans, whom I referred to as blacks. Unfortunately, there was so little mention of individuals in these groups in the contemporary sources that it would have been impossible for me to include them in the kind of analysis I was attempting. This does not mean that I ignored these groups, or that I do not consider them important residents. Rather, it reflects the fact that most Cincinnatians in 1840 viewed their community in terms of its adult white male population, and this vision was reflected in most of the contemporary data I found.

As I developed my analysis, I was surprised to find that nearly half of the adult white male population were boarders, or single young men, many foreign-born, living in large boardinghouses near the river. The census did not identify them by name, but other sources suggested that they were predominantly newcomers who had just arrived in the city, approximately half from Germany. The local press initially welcomed them but soon worried about their effect on the established social order. The boarders contributed to the growth and prosperity of Cincinnati but also played a major role in the cultural, social, and political conflicts that emerged in the pre–Civil War period. I believe the relative size, demographic composition, and distinctive character of this group made it an important part of the story of Cincinnati during the 1840s, one that could have broader implications for our understanding of Jacksonian society and boomtown urbanization.

The other half of the adult white male population of Cincinnati in 1840 were the more established heads of households, who were listed by name in the 1840 census and included, in some cases, in the city directories. They were generally older, native-born, and married, often with families and an established occupation and place of residence.

Tracing a sample of names from the 1840 city directory to preceding directories suggested that many of the differences between the above-mentioned groups of Cincinnatians were related to how long they had lived in the city (what I call priority). In writing about these differences, I made a basic distinction between the heads of households and the transient boarders, and described these groups, graphically, as representing the interior and periphery of a concentric field model of the adult white male population of Cincinnati in 1840. I further differentiated the established members of the city by distinguishing, based on relative length of residence in the city, between old settlers (who formed the core of the field), recent settlers (who were the middle ring), and new settlers (who occupied the outer ring).

This model may seem arbitrary (and perhaps obvious), but it articulates, in many respects, the differences that Cincinnatians saw and felt at this time. They revered their old-timers (the core group) and felt that the respectable community (the middle ring) was being challenged and undermined by the increasing numbers of newcomers (the periphery). In some cases, they described the characteristics of the two groups and estimated their relative size.

During the 1840s, the local press carried stories and editorials about the escalating local conflicts (and the related emergence of two political parties) in Cincinnati based on these kinds of stable-transient, insider-outsider, moral-immoral distinctions. I believe these stories suggest that Cincinnatians at this time thought of their community, implicitly if not explicitly, in terms very similar to this model. More broadly, I think my model could be applied to the analysis of other historical or contemporary communities.

In the third chapter on social structure, I described the occupational composition and wealth distribution of these heads of households in 1840 and traced the changes in their socioeconomic status between 1820 and 1860. The data indicate several trends. Structurally, the community was highly stratified, but there was also considerable fluidity within the system. Individually, most men didn't remain long in the community, but among the minority of men who did, many prospered. This statistical evidence that upward social mobility, or success, resulted from stability is particularly interesting because it reflects a basic tenet of community leaders about the "natural" process of elevation in society.

This analysis of social structure and mobility was very dense (as readers will see if they try to follow it) because it involved a complex set of patterns involving a large number of people. After several years of frustration, I gradually saw the relationship between the demographic and social structure data: the socioeconomic differences within the community represented a vertical dimension to the horizontal concentric field model of the adult white male population. That is, not only could the heads of households in 1840 be classified as old settlers, recent settlers, and new settlers in a horizontal field, but they could also be grouped vertically into social classes based on occupation and property ownership. There was a strong correlation between the horizontal and the vertical dimensions; the result was a three-dimensional conical model, or cone.

This analysis has, I believe, two important general implications. The first is that it confirms the evidence from many other mobility studies documenting the dominant pattern of geographical mobility during the pre–Civil War period: most people seem to have moved from place to place rather than remaining in a single community over time, and unfortunately we can't determine whether they prospered or not. However, I think the second implication is more novel and interesting: that among the minority of people who were geographically stable, there was a dominant pattern of socioeconomic success. Whether this reflects the prevailing opportunities during this period or the special rewards of persistence is open to debate, but it does say something important about the shared experience of people who live together in a place over time.

In the last chapter, on leadership, I returned to my original analysis of the people who participated in voluntary associations in Cincinnati in 1840. I expanded the social analysis and used the conical model to illustrate where the participants fit within the local community. Further, I explored the patterns of participation in different voluntary associations and found a small group of leaders who dominated most of these organizations and represented a kind of "interlocking directorate" (and were largely located in the apex of the cone). Finally, I focused on the social differences between the Democrats and Whigs and found them located in very different sectors of the conical model, which were reflected in their competing political ideologies and concepts of society.

After two decades, I believe this analysis of voluntary associations is still unique and useful. Tocqueville defined the importance of these organizations (in terms very similar to those articulated by several prominent Cincinnatians he met during his visit to the city), but no one has systematically examined their role in the development of a city during this period. Based on my analysis of Cincinnati in 1840, it seems clear that voluntary associations had a major, and probably dominant, role in promoting growth and maintaining order in the community. In many respects, these organizations served as the *instruments* for the economic, cultural, and social interests of a small and stable group of community leaders.

More broadly, I believe my analysis is important because it provides the framework for understanding the basic changes that transformed Cincinnati by midcentury. Around 1840 (and perhaps starting before), the prevailing social order—articulated in the booster spirit, organized through voluntary associations, and representing the interests of the older and more established members of the community—was challenged by the ever-increasing influx of newcomers, particularly Germans, who did not necessarily accept (or even understand) the community ideology and generally did not participate in its organizations. Rather than trying to fit within the community (i.e., following the "natural" process of integration articulated in the gradual movement inside and upward within the conic model), those who stayed, particularly the Germans, developed their own ideas and organizations and used politics to effect fundamental changes. By 1850, through the Democratic Party, they captured control of the city.

In reviewing my manuscript today, I realize that readers may be confused about the time frame of my study: is it limited to 1840 or does it really cover the larger period between 1820 and 1860? As you will see, the primary focus is on 1840 (particularly the detailed analysis of householders used to develop the conic model), but there is also a good deal of evidence (statistical and descriptive) about a broader time frame. For example, to support my argument about the transition from voluntary associations to politics in chapter 4, I used contemporary voting data and city directories to conclude, "As the proportion of the population voting increased—from 8.8% in 1820, to 13.4% in 1840, to 16.5% in 1860—the proportion holding office in formal organizations decreased—from 1.2% in 1820, to .9% in 1840, to .4% in 1860—and the mean number of offices these men held dropped from 1.9 in 1820, to 1.5 in 1840, to 1.2 in 1860."

I realize too that readers may also be confused about *when* Cincinnati changed from the old social order, based on voluntary associations run by the local elite, into the new society, dominated by the two political parties representing competing economic, social, and cultural interests. Clearly, this change occurred gradually over the period 1830 to 1860 and was precipitated by a series of escalating and interrelated local incidents. I believe 1840 was a pivotal time when the old elite and social order still controlled the city but the newcomers were beginning to demand changes. My demographic and social analysis (represented by the conical model), describes the structure of the dominant older community, but the events I describe during this period are indicative of the challenges and eventual capture of the city by the competing new groups.

I began my study of Cincinnati as a case study of Jacksonian America and an attempt to understand the society Tocqueville described in *Democracy in America*. While I have not reviewed the recent academic literature in the field, I believe my analysis provides strong evidence (descriptive as well as statistical) about the character of democratic society and the role of voluntary associations.

Tocqueville stressed the excesses or dangers of egalitarianism; when I wrote this book, his view had come to be accepted as the prevailing pattern in Jacksonian America. I believed, however, that Tocqueville ignored the more interesting relationship between the "masses" and "men of talent," which Cincinnatians described for him in 1831, and this is evident in my analysis of the population in 1840. At this time, at least in Cincinnati, the two groups coexisted in relative harmony (although this broke down with the gradual shift from elite to mass control over the pre–Civil War period).

Tocqueville also stressed the importance of voluntary associations and how they were used to promote democratic interests. Here, too, at least in Cincinnati, the evidence suggests that while they played a major role in the development of the city, they served more as agents of elite social control at the time of his visit (although there was also a gradual shift to political parties as agents of the class and cultural interests).

The point here is not that Tocqueville misrepresented American society in the 1830s (at least in describing Cincinnati), rather, it is to suggest he was able to anticipate future trends (and found Cincinnati to be particularly instructive). However, at least for Cincinnati, which, according to Tocqueville, was more advanced than the rest of America, the democratic excesses Tocqueville described and that are generally assumed to have been prevalent in Jacksonian America, did not become dominant until midcentury.

Finally, what, if any, value does this study of Cincinnati in 1840 have for people studying urbanization and the character of historical or contemporary cities? I would assume that the general themes I have described here may be found in other cities at this time or boomtowns in other periods but, in every case, they are unique to that particular place and time. However, I would assert that the conceptual framework and analytical model I developed here can be applied elsewhere and that it will be useful in understanding the dynamics of boomtown urbanization and the social and functional organization of cities.

Introduction

⤫

The Jacksonian Urban Community

We are very pleased with the visit we have just made to Cincinnati, it was most interesting. . . . All that there is of good or of bad in American society is to be found there in such strong relief that one would be tempted to call it one of those books printed in large letters for teaching children to read; everything there is in violent contrast, exaggerated; nothing has fallen into its final place: society is growing more rapidly than man.
—ALEXIS DE TOCQUEVILLE, 1831

Alexis de Tocqueville in Cincinnati

In December 1831 the French traveler Alexis de Tocqueville visited Cincinnati. Stepping ashore from his steamboat, Tocqueville saw a "singular spectacle." Here was a city which "seem[ed] to want to rise too quickly for people to have any system or plan about it. Great buildings, thatched cottages, streets encumbered with debris, houses under construction, no names on the streets, no numbers on the houses, no outward luxury, but the image of industry and labor obvious at every step."[1]

Tocqueville spent nearly four days in the Queen City. In this booming young western metropolis he could observe the spectacle of democracy in action. As he mingled with the people on the streets, Tocqueville overheard their animated conversations, noted their effusive habits, and imbibed the heady egalitarian atmosphere. Interviewing some of the leading members of the local society, Tocqueville heard many proud stories about the rise of the young metropolis. He asked questions about the development of judicial, educational, and penal institutions and traded guarded criticisms of the excesses of democracy.

Repeatedly, talk turned to the topic of the pervasive power of the people. "We have carried Democracy to its last limits," declared Salmon P. Chase, the young lawyer from New Hampshire who would become Lincoln's secretary of the treasury and chief justice of the Supreme Court during Reconstruction. "We have yielded too much to Democracy here" was the comment of Bellamy Storer, prominent local attorney, reformer, and Whig politician. "Our Democracy is without limits," agreed Cincinnati's foremost physician, Daniel Drake. "We are at this moment trying out a Democracy without limits; everything is going that way," concluded Timothy Walker, a young Harvard graduate who had just settled in the city. "But shall we be able to endure it? As yet no one can say positively."[2]

Since these criticisms confirmed Tocqueville's own preconceptions about American society, they made a strong impression on him, and he emphasized the excesses and dangers of egalitarianism in his analysis *Democracy in America.* In doing so, however, he ignored or minimized the import of Chase's remark that "in spite of everything, it's still the influence of men of talent which rules us." Tocqueville also failed to take into account the fact that he was immediately able to identify the most prominent men in the community and that they were widely recognized as its outstanding citizens and spokesmen. Finally, he disregarded the evidence of the illustrious careers and reputations of his informants. These men were all highly successful, highly respected, and influential leaders in Cincinnati. Their success, prestige, and power offered dramatic proof that a civilized, accomplished elite could exist within this new egalitarian society.[3]

The Masses and the Men of Talent

According to Tocqueville, and many other contemporary observers, the second quarter of the nineteenth century was a period of rapid social change, in which the new masses challenged and defeated the older men of talent, and rampant democracy shattered the traditional deferential social order. After the outstanding achievement of the Revolutionary generation—the native-born aristocracy of ability and experience who guided the young republic through the perilous years of independence, confederation, and constitution-making—such men of talent gradually lost their commanding position in American life. The fiasco of the Hartford Convention, the demise of the Federalist Party, and the successive deaths of the Republican statesmen and Revolutionary heroes left the country without a strong, aggressive, responsible elite.

The election of Andrew Jackson in 1828, in this analysis, signaled the rise of the masses and the triumph of raw democracy. Through the extension of the franchise, the creation of new economic opportunities, and the opening of the West, the common man rode roughshod across America. In the process, under the acid influence of democracy, the established values and deferential social order of the older generation were diluted or dissolved, and Americans lived together in a kind of natural anarchy.[4]

The consequences for man and society, according to this interpretation, were disastrous. For Tocqueville, democracy meant the leveling of society and the absence of extremes of wealth and poverty, power and impotence, knowledge and ignorance, but the result was a pervasive mediocrity in the quality of life. A broad diffusion of competence was gained at the cost of individual cases of excellence. Individualism—the term Tocqueville used to describe the condition of man in this new egalitarian society—resulted in isolation and loneliness for the individual. Competent and confident in his own ability, refusing to admit superior knowledge or experience in any of his fellow men, the individual turned within himself with a kind of anarchic self-reliance. Equality of condition thereby precluded the possibility of a stable, cohesive society with a responsible, effective elite.

This analysis rests on certain basic assumptions about the character and quality of life in America during the second quarter of the nineteenth century. It assumes the general irrelevance of tradition, background, experience, or ability in the routine of daily life or the structure of society. It also assumes the presence of generous opportunities for economic achievement and social success, the prevalence and importance of mobility—in status as well as residence—and a general pattern of accomplishment and rising status for individuals. Further, it assumes a democratic society in which a substantial majority of men held property, voted, participated in public affairs, and belonged to some ill-defined but ascendant middle class. Finally, this analysis assumes that these conditions made social stability and cohesion impossible, and that the dominance of the masses precluded the possibility of any influential role for the men of talent.

The central thesis of this analysis of American society during the pre–Civil War years was expressed succinctly by Tocqueville's traveling companion, Gustave de Beaumont, soon after their arrival in Cincinnati. "The character of this society," wrote Beaumont, "is that of having none." Certainly there was good reason for observers like Tocqueville and Beaumont, accustomed and inclined to an old, settled, deferential form of society, to have this reaction. Everything in America—the conditions, customs, and character—was new to them. The novelty of the experience emphasized the extreme aspects of the society, which, along with their personal prejudices and preconceptions, undoubtedly distorted their perception and analysis of American society.

Moreover, when Tocqueville visited America in 1831, the country had just gone through a major transition, which had been a traumatic experience for many citizens. The election of Andrew Jackson seemed to many Americans, especially the "better sort," to mark the end of a noble experiment and the beginning of anarchy. Perhaps at no other time during the first half of the nineteenth century were men of genteel background, education, and eminence so disturbed and doubtful about the validity or future of the republic. Their fears, poured forth to such sympathetic listeners as Tocqueville and Beaumont, doubtless compounded the negative and hostile impressions of these young Frenchmen.

The subsequent popularity of this view of the Jacksonian period results from the influence of *Democracy in America* and the common assumptions of older historians. The brilliance of insight, cogency of argument, and contemporary appeal of the analysis have made *Democracy in America* one of the most important and widely accepted interpretations of the Jacksonian period. Despite the obvious distortions of the argument, reflecting the author's strong prejudices and preconceptions, *Democracy in America* has been accepted as an incisive analysis of Jacksonian society.

Moreover, until recently, historians generally accepted as fact the ascendance of democracy during the second quarter of the nineteenth century, the concomitant breakdown of society, and the demise of a deferential social order. Both those who welcomed the triumph of the common man and those who deplored the loss of order and leadership agreed that this was, in fact, what happened.

The question remains, however, whether this was the true state of society during the Jacksonian period. What exactly was the relationship between the masses and the men of talent, and were the two groups necessarily incompatible? Was Salmon P. Chase's statement "We have carried democracy to its last limits" a more accurate description of the prevailing conditions than his remark "In spite of everything, it's still the influence of men of talent that rules us," and are these two necessarily mutually exclusive? More important, was Beaumont right in saying that "the character of this society is that of having none," that Americans lived in some kind of unstructured, unstable state of nature?

Timothy Walker on Cincinnati Society

One of Tocqueville's most "important" informants in Cincinnati, he wrote in his diary, and underlined, was Timothy Walker. At twenty-nine, three years older than Tocqueville, this Harvard graduate arrived in the Queen City in the summer of 1830. He originally intended to stay for only a year in order to gain admission to the Ohio Bar, which in lieu of seven years of apprenticeship at home, would permit him to practice law in Massachusetts. But he soon became infatuated with the thriving Ohio River metropolis and decided to stay in the West. Armed with a Harvard diploma and fortified by a good mind and Yankee self-assurance, Walker soon had a prosperous law practice and became a prominent member of the local society. Described as "one of those universal men who will grow mighty in any soil," Walker secured his position in 1832 when he "married $50,000 *and* a very interesting damsel."[5]

Walker, like Chase, described for Tocqueville the power of the masses and the excesses of democracy, and expressed some fears about how American democracy might end up. But he, too, was basically optimistic and enthusiastic about the character of the community and the quality of local life. In his description Walker may have repeated or referred to comments on the subject he had written for the *New England Magazine* the preceding fall. In his "Letter from Ohio," Walker presented a classic description of the new western society and an analysis that closely anticipated Tocqueville's.[6]

In this short article the young New England emigrant recorded his initial impressions of Cincinnati. He first commented on the beautiful natural setting of the city, "where nature performed her *chef d'oeuvre*"; the young and enterprising inhabitants, whose maxim was "*possunt quia posse videntur*—they can prevail because they think they can"; and the marvelous prospects of the western city. He warned his Boston friends that unless they quickened their pace, the Queen City would soon bypass the proud Yankee center. Walker made no effort to impress his readers with the literary institutions, the public monuments, or the polished manners of the citizens, for he readily admitted they had none. But "for native resolution, sound practical sense, clear perceptions of expediency, prevailing frugality, and untiring activity," he concluded, "I know not where to look for a superior."

Turning to the structure of the society, Walker wrote: "If you ask who among us are lions, I shall be obliged to answer, all or none. We have few trees towering much above the rest, and hold to the doctrine of equality most pertinaciously. The upright man is the gentleman, no matter what his calling." In this "free and easy" society, Walker continued, "all power is in the hands of the people, and never did the miser guard his treasure with greater vigilance. To use the homely but significant phrase, every man stands upon his own bottom. . . . Standing thus alone, and unallied, our motto in action is 'each for himself, and heaven for us all.'" Thus, in 1830, before Tocqueville arrived in America, Walker found in Cincinnati what would soon be called "individualism." His description of this quality could hardly be improved upon by Tocqueville: "Necessity teaches us to be self-confident and self-dependent; and probably no people abound more in moral courage, which sometimes degenerates into modest assurance. This keeps the individual from being merged with the mass, and furnishes ample occasion for developing the strongest traits of character."[7]

And yet, unlike Tocqueville, Walker did not foresee mediocrity as the result of this egalitarian climate. As he wrote in 1837:

> Where the actual equality of condition approaches so nearly to the theoretical equality of rights—where, instead of here and there an overgrown fortune, glaring out from the midst of general poverty, we see some very rich and some very poor, but all commanding the necessities of life, and looking forward gradually to its luxuries—the leveling disposition will work upward, instead of downward. The many may strive to elevate themselves, rather than to pull down the few who happen to be above them; and in a free and generous competition, the whole will press onward and upward.

Instead of some irreconcilable conflict between the masses and the men of talent, Walker argued that it was possible for everyone to improve themselves and that the combined success of these individuals was, in fact, the foundation of social progress.[8]

Despite their recognition of the democratic character of Cincinnati society, men like Walker and Chase did not fear the Jacobinical excesses that plagued Tocqueville's mind. Instead, they emphasized the friendly, open spirit of the community, enjoyed the economic opportunities it offered, and soon emerged as successful, influential members of the local establishment. Their concern over the "excesses" of the masses, their criticism of some "democracy without limits," was largely political, a caustic reference to the success of a popular young candidate for Congress. They complained that the populace made bad choices in elections but did not question the people's right to vote. Rather than a conflict between the excesses of the masses and the authority of the men of talent, Chase and Walker saw an opportunity to allow both to develop, constructively, in a growing community.

Cincinnati as Microcosm

During the years before the Civil War, Cincinnati was one of the largest and most rapidly growing urban centers in the United States, a city that interested not only local partisans and visitors from abroad but anyone concerned with the American scene. In a period of extremely self-conscious introspection by Americans and excessive probing by foreigners for the elusive key to the national character, the Queen City was a popular subject of study. Drawn from all parts of the Union and many European countries, having faced many of the peculiarly American conditions of the frontier, Cincinnatians, according to many contemporary commentators, formed a virtual microcosm of American society.

With the founding of the community in 1788, Cincinnati established a strategic position along the main channel of westward expansion, the Ohio River, and soon emerged as the preeminent metropolis of the trans-Appalachian region. Within the course of a generation, by 1820, the small frontier outpost had grown into a prosperous trading center of over ten thousand residents; within another generation, by 1850, it had become a diversified metropolis of over one hundred thousand, the fifth largest city and the second largest manufacturing center in the United States. During the seven decades preceding the Civil War no other American city experienced such a spectacular rise, and few entertained such splendid ambitions for future growth and greatness. Cincinnati was, indeed, the first of the great boom cities of the nineteenth century, preceding Chicago, Denver, and Los Angeles.

During these years the Queen City was an exciting, dynamic community. In every decade of the first half of the nineteenth century the population doubled, or better, due largely to the large influx of immigrants from the eastern states and Europe who came to realize their dreams in this western metropolis. Here they found a vibrant economy based initially on river commerce but, during the 1830s and 1840s, increasingly on manufacturing. In a young community like this—where a man's present accomplishments were more important than his prior advantages, where ability and a "go-ahead" spirit were of more value than a distinguished background and social graces—opportunity attracted the most ambitious and enterprising young men of their generation.

And yet the dramatic success of the Queen City depended not only on the influx of enterprising immigrants but also on the emergence of social organization and effective leadership. The remarkable development of the city was the result of the coordinated efforts of Cincinnatians and the high quality of community leadership. It reflects, fundamentally, the successful molding of a sense of common identity and commitment within a large and rapidly growing population which, when translated into concerted action, benefited the community as a whole. Social order, therefore, was as important as individual opportunity in the success of Cincinnati.

This spectacular success of the Queen City—its rapid growth and widespread popularity—made it the subject of intensive analysis. Usually the comments were favorable, as with such distinguished visitors as Harriet Martineau, Charles Dickens, and Horace Greeley; sometimes, as with Mrs. Trollope, the comments were highly critical. But in either case, the attention on Cincinnati reflected its contemporary importance. The Queen City was, indeed, as Tocqueville noted, a good place to study American society in the Jacksonian period.

A Community Profile

In order to understand the conditions of the Jacksonian urban society—both the conditions as they actually existed and the ways in which contemporary observers perceived them—it is helpful to study a single community intensively for a limited period of time. Such a microscopic analysis, which uses all of the many diverse sources available, both qualitative and quantitative, makes it possible to examine more deeply the character and conditions of a city than has hitherto been possible. The resulting community profile can also suggest the general character of urban society during the years preceding the Civil War.[9]

The following analysis of Cincinnati in 1840 is an attempt to re-create the social organization of the city by using many of the official quantitative records along with the standard qualitative sources. Certain methods are developed for the analysis of the city as a functional social system, contemporary social concepts are employed, and a paradigm for community profiles that could be used in comparative studies is suggested.

The year 1840 serves as the focal point of this study for two reasons: first, because there is a great wealth and variety of data from the years 1838 to 1842 necessary for such a study, and second, because 1840 seems to represent a critical point in the development of the city. With the tremendous growth of the population, the large influx of German immigrants, and the emergence of industry as the leading component of the local economy during the fifteen years following 1835, Cincinnati gradually evolved from a relatively small, homogeneous, cohesive community with a clearly defined set of values and sense of purpose into a large, heterogeneous, divisive metropolis fraught with internal strife and conflicting ambitions.

In 1840 Cincinnati retained, at least on the surface, much of the appearance and character of its earlier stage of development. However, below the surface, forces were at work that would propel the city in the coming years into its second stage of development. The purpose of this study is not to describe or explain the changes that occurred in the years before the Civil War but to analyze some of the conditions that contributed to it. Because some knowledge of developments before and after 1840 is necessary to put the present study into historical perspective, however, a short discussion of the history of Cincinnati up to 1840 opens the study and a short discussion of major changes after 1840 closes the book.

Four aspects of the social organization of the community—its ideology, demography, social structure, and leadership—form the heart of this study, each of which is the focus of a chapter. The early history of Cincinnati is presented as the local boosters described it to promote a sense of special community identity. The demographic character of the 1840 population is articulated in terms of relative differences in length of adult residence in the city. The social structure of the community is reconstructed and explained in terms of a dynamic model. Finally, the role of voluntary associations, the character of the leaders, and their involvement and influence in the organizational life of the community are analyzed in order to demonstrate their central role in the functional structure of the city.

This analysis suggests that, despite considerable demographic volatility and heterogeneity and a highly stratified social structure, the ideology of progress and prosperity gave the community a sense of common identity, and the local leadership provided the necessary organization and direction. These conditions underlay the dramatic development of the city during the 1840s, but they also contributed to the changes that occurred around 1850, when Cincinnati began to lose its momentum and confidence and became increasingly preoccupied by internal conflicts and fragmentation. These changes, manifest in political developments during the 1840s and 1850s, were largely the result of the dynamics of population growth during this period.

The Sources and Methodology

Sources for this analysis of Cincinnati in 1840 are the United States Census of 1840 for Hamilton County (City of Cincinnati), the 1838 Tax List for Cincinnati, David Shaffer's *Cincinnati Directory for 1840,* Charles Cist's guidebook *Cincinnati in 1841,* the seven daily newspapers printed during this period, several standard local histories, and the large collection of biographical and manuscript material available at the Cincinnati Historical Society.

In the following discussion a distinction will be made between the population of 13,705 adult white males, and the smaller group of 8,684 householders. The former group includes all men in Cincinnati at the time of the census, including a good number of transient rivermen, migrants, and recently arrived immigrants who were not fully settled or integrated into the life of the community. The latter group includes most of the stable citizens, men with families, steady jobs, and established residences, who had been in the city long enough to feel some commitment to the community. The householders, therefore, represent the more permanent, stable, and responsible element within the total population of the city. In the following discussion of the total adult white male population of the city, information will be taken from the United States Census; in the discussion of the settled, established householders, however, information will be taken from the *Directory for 1840.*[10]

The *Directory for 1840,* surveyed and published by David H. Shaffer in late 1839, includes the names of 8,684 male residents. It indicates the nativity, residence, and occupation of these householders. Because of the considerable number of male householders included in the *Directory for 1840,* sampling techniques were necessary. In order to get a general profile of the character and composition of the householders, every tenth name was drawn from the directory, producing what will be called the Shaffer sample of 868 male householders, which, from several independent tests, appears to have been fairly representative of the total Shaffer population. This Shaffer sample provides the basis for generalizations concerning the character and composition of the Cincinnati community in 1840.

Information on the associational activities of Cincinnatians is derived from membership rosters, local newspaper lists, Shaffer's *Directory for 1840* and Cist's *Cincinnati in 1841.* During this period, at least in Cincinnati, the newspapers regularly published articles on the activities of various informal associations—meetings, committees, and other groups—including a listing of the names of many of the participants. By copying the lists from the seven different newspapers active during the three-year period 1839–42, an extensive and varied collection of voluntary associations was assembled. These lists were then indexed to make a file of the 1,050 participants whose names appeared on these lists at least once. Cist's *Cincinnati in 1841* and Shaffer's *Directory for 1840* both included sections on the major formal organizations in the city during this period, with lists of their officers. These formal organizations included banks and insurance companies, and the officials of the local government. The result was a file of the 396 men who held offices in Cincinnati's formal organizations. Together, these two files of men active in local informal and formal associations include all of the 1,194 *activists* in the community between 1839 and 1842.

In the following discussion, *participation* refers to any newspaper evidence of involvement by an individual in some meeting, committee, or other informal group. Sometimes it was the result of having spoken at a meeting or served on a committee; at other times it resulted from the signing of a petition or statement; and in some cases the criteria for inclusion in a list are unknown. These lists clearly did not include the names of every citizen who attended such meetings or served on such committees, nor do they always indicate the character of interest or involvement, but they may be taken to provide a fairly accurate and comprehensive basic index of personal participation in informal associations.

Power will be used in the following discussion to designate the holding of an office in a formal organization, such as bank director, city councilman, masonic officer, or school trustee. While the character of the men holding these offices differed greatly, as did their ability and sense of responsibility, these men were, by virtue of their names appearing regularly in the newspapers or in the directory or guidebook, the most visible and clearly defined leadership group in the community.[11]

The activists include the 1,194 male householders who participated in some informal group or held power in some formal organization, or both, during the three-year period 1839–42. Participation and power are separate, but not unrelated, manifestations of associational activity; the latter is assumed to represent a greater degree of involvement and influence than the former because of the more lasting and clearly defined character of the activity. In order to measure the extent of involvement and influence of each activist throughout the total network of voluntary associations, the number of different categories of informal and formal associations in which he is active is totaled, with participation in each of the eight categories of formal organizations counting two acts. This combined "index of associational activity" indicates not the intensity of commitment within each category of voluntary associations but rather the extent of activity across the total associational network.[12]

The men with the highest indexes of associational activity are considered to be the "associational elite" of the community because they were most extensively involved and influential in the network of voluntary associations. In order to determine whether these men were generally recognized as community leaders—to establish a rough measure of their prestige as well as their participation and power—the Biographical Indexes of the Cincinnati Historical Society are used. These indexes to all biographical references in Charles Theodore Greve's *History of Cincinnati* and several other standard works written during the nineteenth century suggest whether these men achieve some permanent place in the history of the city. Inclusion in these indexes indicates that an individual was considered by contemporary authorities of Cincinnati history to have been among the most prominent Cincinnatians at this time.[13]

Certainly, the newspapers did not report every group that appeared in the community, nor did the names of participants include every citizen who was involved in these groups. Similarly, the directory and guidebook did not include all of the associations that existed between 1839 and 1842, or the names of all of their officers. But a check against other sources—general histories, associational records, biographies, and manuscript collections—suggests that most of the major associations were reported, and that these sources included, in most cases, the names of the prominent and active participants and officers in these groups. The most important possible omission was German immigrant associations, formed in the late 1830s, which were generally not reported in the English-language press (or in the German press). The striking fact about these newspaper lists, Shaffer's *Directory for 1840,* and *Cincinnati in 1841,* however, is the remarkably comprehensive character of their information concerning the organization and operation of associations in the city.

Moreover, because of their widespread circulation and semipublic character, these sources had a kind of legitimizing function: inclusion in their pages not only reflected the importance of voluntary associations but also helped to publicize their activities and influence. The inclusion of voluntary associations in the newspapers, guidebooks, and directories, therefore represents a contemporary criterion of their relative importance and recognition within the community and provides a convenient common standard for a study of associational activity in Cincinnati in 1840.

A Functional Model of the Community

From these sources and methods, a functional model of Cincinnati in 1840 evolved based on relative differences in the degree of individual *identity* and *involvement* within the community. Identity is determined by inclusion in the city directory; it establishes the presence of an individual and the social characteristics that help to define his relative position within the community. Involvement is determined by inclusion in the newspaper, guidebook, and directory associational lists; it establishes the form and extent of an individual's participation and power in voluntary associations that suggests his relative influence in local affairs. An analysis of the Cincinnati community in 1840 based on identity and involvement indicates the structural relationship between individuals in terms of their organization within a functioning social system.

The validity of this approach rests on two fundamental assumptions: first, that in a large, complex, and increasingly impersonal city like Cincinnati, social interaction and integration required the kind of personal visibility and publicity that this identity represented; second, that in a period when voluntary associations were the most common means of group enterprise, community interests and influence were achieved through the kind of participation and power that this involvement represented. The following analysis, therefore, assumes that Cincinnati was a functioning social system organized and operated according to the degree of citizen identity and involvement represented in these sources.

This analytic framework is used to reconstruct the general organization and operation of the community. Analyzing the demographic character and composition of the adult white male population shows that its remarkable volatility, variety, and vitality were described and interpreted by Cincinnatians in terms of relative differences in the length of residence, or *priority,* in the city. Priority, then, reflects other differences in age, family, status, nativity, and psychological identification with the community that are central to an understanding of its social organization.

Second, the socioeconomic class structure is described, based on analysis of the economic and occupational differences among the householders, and related to the major demographic divisions in order to show that these differences must be evaluated within the context of an open and evolving social system. Finally, an analysis of participation and power in voluntary associations demonstrates that associational activity was limited to a minority of householders, and that the broad range of involvement and influence of a small group of well-established, successful activists was a manifestation of their elite position in the community.

This analysis implies that there were three separate but related components of the 1840 adult white male population, each of which had a distinctive role within the functional social system. (1) Approximately a third of the men were in an unsettled underclass composed primarily of recent German immigrants and transient rivermen. As workers and consumers, these newcomers contributed greatly to the city's growth and prosperity, but as single young men, generally without families or homes, they had little other contact with the more established householders and seemed to threaten the prevailing social order. (2) Over half of the men formed a silent middle class composed of householders who arrived in the city sometime during the 1830s and had, by 1840, established homes, families, and jobs. As mechanics and shopkeepers, they represented the backbone of the local economy, but as new or recent settlers in the community, they did not yet have the time or experience to own property or to take an active part in local affairs. (3) Less than a sixth of the men belonged to the well-established active, elite composed of the older, successful householders who had been in the city for at least a decade and had had the time and experience necessary to obtain positions of community leadership. As the leading local professionals, merchants, and manufacturers in the community, they directed its economic development, while as property owners, they benefited from its continued growth and prosperity.

These three population components were loosely bound together into a functioning social system by the community ideology. The promise of continued progress and prosperity, and the strong socializing influence of local institutions, helped to unite the population and maintain social order. This ideology exaggerated, no doubt, the conditions of harmony and well-being, but it served as an effective means of attracting and integrating newcomers and provided a sense of cohesion and direction for the rapidly expanding city. This ideology was articulated by the local elite and served their interests, but as long as the city continued to grow it seemed to satisfy the large majority of Cincinnatians as well.

These common values and goals were translated into reality through voluntary associations. It was through associational activity that individuals joined together to form various groups that improved and expanded their personal experience. It was within the total network of these voluntary associations that most local affairs were transacted, because the associations represented the broadest network of contacts, communication, and cooperation within the city. Although voluntary associations were less important in the lives of most Cincinnatians than family, friends, neighborhood, or place of work, and less important in the general growth and prosperity of the city than the larger political and social conditions of the outside world or the economic resources and productivity of the local workforce, they formed the central nexus for a variety of activities in the ongoing life of the community. Voluntary associations provided the central institutional context for community development.

An Analytic Framework for Urban History

In recent years, American urban historians have turned from a formal, comprehensive description of events and institutions in particular cities to a more limited but systematic analysis of particular social problems and processes within the urban environment. This "new urban history" has produced a number of important studies of the problems of urban housing, poverty, welfare, and reform and the processes of residential and occupational mobility. Because these studies have focused on particular social problems and processes rather than on the general urban context in which they occurred, however, they are more properly "social" than "urban" history. A broad analytic framework for the study of cities as distinctive, important contexts of social change remains to be developed.[14]

Over a century ago, in 1854, Richard Hildreth suggested the importance of urbanization in American development: "Density of population, and the existence of towns and cities," he wrote, "are essential to any great degree of social progress." His description of cities as "the central points from which knowledge, enterprise, and civilization stream out upon the surrounding country" suggests their significance in American history. Subsequently, two of the most influential American historians, Frederick Jackson Turner and Charles Beard, both realized the importance of urban development, but their focus was never directly on cities and their framework was more descriptive than analytical. Arthur M. Schlesinger, taking up Turner's challenge to "do a paper on the significance of the City in American History" in 1940, could only describe the rise of cities and their increasing role in national development. William Diamond, in a critique of Schlesinger's essay, pointed out the analytical limitations of this historical approach and suggested that historians turn to the works of urban sociologists for inspiration.[15]

In response to Schlesinger's call for a greater emphasis on the study of cities, American historians published a number of solid urban biographies and monographs on the economic, institutional, and political development of cities, but the only useful analytic contributions were Richard Wade's comparative approach, and several general reviews of the problems and possibilities inherent in urban history. Eric Lampard's essay "American Historians and the Study of Urbanization" challenged his colleagues to turn from the study of "problems" in cities to urbanization as a "societal process" and suggested the utility of a broad, comparative demographic and ecological framework. This essay was more widely read than understood, or followed, but Lampard later reviewed his argument and expanded his analytic framework to include: (1) the population, (2) the topography, (3) the economy, (4) the social organization, (5) the political process, (6) the civic leadership, and (7) the civic culture, realized largely through voluntary associations; (8) external relations, (9) the "image" of the city, and (10) the process of city building and (11) the legal integument, which place the preceding into a dynamic context.[16]

Lampard's argument draws on an extensive knowledge of the social science literature on urbanization; like Diamond thirty years earlier, he seems to be encouraging historians to develop a broader and more comparative framework for their study of cities. Although the available historical information about cities varies from place to place and from period to period, and is never as detailed or comprehensive as that included in contemporary social surveys, various concepts and methods of social scientists can be adopted, or adapted, by historians in order to interpret evidence about a particular city and put it into a broader comparative framework. A review of some of the classic statements on the city, the newer social systems theory of the functional organization of communities, and the findings of some of the community studies suggests one possible framework for the historical analysis of cities.

In his classic essay "Urbanism as a Way of Life," Louis Wirth defined a city as a "relatively large, dense, and permanent settlement of socially heterogeneous individuals." Although Wirth described the depersonalizing influence of urbanization as making primary relationships "superficial," "transitory," and "segmental," he also noted the concomitant rise of voluntary associations, the great variety of secondary relationships urbanites form in order to pursue their common interests and needs. In a later definition of urbanism, Albert J. Reiss listed some of its distinguishing characteristics: "(a) A complex division of labor with a diversified occupational structure which forms a major basis of the system of social stratification; (b) high territorial and social mobility; (c) marked functional dependence of the population; (d) substantial personal anonymity in interpersonal contacts and segmentalization of social roles and role interactions; (e) reliance on indirect modes of social control; (f) normative deviance." Both Wirth and Reiss emphasize the importance of population concentration and the major behavioral and structural consequences that result in a distinctive form of social organization.[17]

The description and analysis of this distinctive form of social organization is one of the main concerns of community studies. Definitions of community vary considerably, but most include the following components: (1) demographic—a territorially defined population; (2) psychological—shared values and goals; and (3) sociological—structural and functional interdependence. In a sense, therefore, all communities may be conceived of as social systems, defined by Charles P. Loomis as being "composed of the patterned interaction of members," and, more generally, as a set of patterned relationships between structural or functional groups within the population. They may also be conceived of as social networks, which anthropologists use to describe ties between individuals in small groups, or communications networks, which represent highly sophisticated, quantitative models for input-output analysis.[18]

The critical problem of translating these conceptual models of the community into a meaningful, manageable research design has best been resolved, perhaps, by Harold Kaufman, who proposes an "interactional conception of community." Kaufman's point is that there are many different interactional fields within the geographically defined territory of the community, but only a portion of the total body of community phenomena are "communally relevant": "The community field consists of an organization of actions carried on by persons working through various associations or groups. This organization of actions occupies the center of the community arena and is distinguished from other fields of action in a locality by a complex of characteristics or dimensions." This kind of analysis, according to Kaufman, requires an emphasis on three particular elements of community action: the persons involved as participants in the action, the associations or groups through which the actions take place, and the stages or periods of action through time. Unfortunately, there are no full-scale empirical studies using this approach, but the evidence drawn from other community studies can be incorporated into this analytic model.[19]

Studies of the extent of organized participation in communities indicate that most Americans belong to some organizations, but that the proportion varies considerably with the definition of voluntary associations, the size and character of communities, and the different groups in the population. In a summary of much of this research, David L. Sills found that the proportion of the population affiliated with some voluntary association varied from two-thirds, in Burlington, Vermont, Chicago, and Detroit, to a third, in Newburyport, Westchester County, and Maryland, but that most of the people affiliated belonged to only one organization and were not active in its affairs, and that a relatively settled, educated, successful, and urbanized minority of interested citizens dominated most voluntary associations.[20]

A number of studies have analyzed patterns of associational activity in order to describe the leadership structure and identify the power elite in different communities. In a survey of this literature, Charles M. Bonjean and David M. Olson have pointed out that the very different conclusions of these studies, particularly between those that find an elitist or a pluralist structure, are closely related to their selection of a positional, reputational, or decisional method of analysis. In a major study combining several of these approaches, Robert Presthus has argued that the "scope of a leader's activity" is the best indication of his relative power, and that the proportion of leaders with multiple, or overlapping, areas of activity is the best comparable "index of elitism." Reviewing a number of community power studies, Presthus concludes that the elite represent approximately 1% of each population, but that the proportion of overlapping activity, which ranged from 52% in Kenosha, Wisconsin, to 6% in New Haven, Connecticut, was roughly inverse to the size of the total population, and reflects the process of specialization, hence pluralism, associated with urbanization.[21]

There have also been a number of attempts by different social scientists to develop a conceptual framework within which variations in leadership structures can be described and interpreted in relation to other community characteristics. In a statistical analysis of 166 American communities, attempting to relate leadership structure with community size and social composition, Claire W. Gilbert found that newer cities with younger populations and a higher rate of growth tended to be elitist while larger and more demographically stable cities were characteristically pluralistic. In a theoretical essay on community decision-making structure, Terry N. Clark has hypothesized that the larger and more heterogeneous a community's population, the greater the potential for interlocking memberships and crosscutting status sets but, paradoxically, the less dense the crosscutting status sets, which contribute to the control of community conflict.[22]

Unfortunately, there have been relatively few historical studies of changing patterns of community power structures. Robert Dahl's analysis of the social characteristics of the mayors of New Haven from 1784 to 1953 describes a gradual shift from an "oligarchy to pluralism," and several other studies have demonstrated a similar historical process of elite loss of control of local government. Lloyd Warner's attempt to project a strong, stable Yankee elite into Newburyport's past, however, has been shown by Stephen Thernstrom to be methodologically unjustified and historically inaccurate. And Robert O. Schultze, in a study of the power structure of Ypsilanti, Michigan, between 1832 and 1955, has traced the gradual "withdrawal of the economic dominants from active and overt participation in public life."[23]

Together, this social science literature suggests a general framework for the analysis of historical cities. As mentioned earlier, when looking at the city as a community, it is necessary to emphasize the three components—demographic, psychological, and sociological—defined on p. 18. These three characteristics are represented in the following discussion in the chapters on ideology (shared values and goals), demography (a territorially defined population), social structure (structural interdependence), and leadership (functional interdependence).

Using Kaufman's interactional concept of the community, it is possible to consider associational activity as communally relevant action. By focusing on voluntary associations as the institutions through which local affairs are organized and operated, the community can be analyzed as a dynamic functioning social system. Such analysis, according to Kaufman, would emphasize three elements: (1) the persons involved as participants in the action, (2) the associations or groups through which the actions take place, and (3) the stages or periods of actions over time. This analytic framework, which is roughly comparable to that of many contemporary community studies, allows the historian to investigate the extent of citizen participation in local affairs, the composition and form of local leadership, and the changes in the leadership and structure over time.

Broadly conceived, this framework allows the historian to incorporate most, if not all, of the elements Eric Lampard suggested are necessary in urban historical analysis. Chapter 1 discusses the image of the city, the process of city building, and, in a general sense, the civic culture. Because this ideology also depended, indirectly, on contemporary perceptions of the topography and the economy, this chapter also includes a review of these elements. Chapter 2 describes the population, chapter 3 details the social organization, and chapter 4 deals with the civic leadership, and, to some degree, the political process in Cincinnati. Although my analysis excludes external relations and the legal integument, it provides a fairly broad and comprehensive framework for the historical analysis of cities.

Finally, contemporary community studies literature suggests a general hypothesis about the structural development of cities. Although most of these studies are cross-sectional rather than longitudinal, the fact that they describe communities of different sizes and during different stages of growth makes it possible to derive from them a general model of historical development. Each community has a distinctive ideology, demography, social structure, and leadership, but these differences can be related, roughly, to particular stages of structural evolution. During this process, at least for communities that go through an early stage of rapid population growth, a relatively small power elite with broad, compatible interests forms and effectively promotes development. Gradually, however, rapid growth and increased size undercut their ability to control and direct continued change, and eventually, in the new and expanded city, a pluralist coalition takes over and exploits the prevailing conflicts and chaos in order to pursue its own interests.

It is this critical stage of transition—the conditions that lead up to it, the dynamics of the complex process, and the various consequences of this pattern of development—that is central to an understanding of urbanization. The distinguishing characteristics of the preceding and succeeding period are relatively clear, and are suggested in the many classic descriptions of the community-society dichotomy, but the critical transitional process has yet to be described. A systematic analysis of cities as functional social systems, and particularly of the structural changes that occur during this transitional process, could lead the urban historian out of the restrictions of a particular subject—isolated in time and space— into the more challenging area of comparative social analysis. It would provide the framework necessary to make detailed, comprehensive comparisons over an extended period of time, and among different cities, that could transform a set of disparate urban histories into a synthetic survey of urbanization.[24]

Finally, this approach would help resolve the question whether the history of cities can be understood better within the framework of distinctive stages of development common to most, if not all, cities during a particular period of their natural history, or conversely, within the framework of the broad periods of national history, during which all cities, irrespective of their particular size or character, experienced certain common problems and changes. The answer to this question, which ultimately will incorporate elements of both, should provide a more solid basis for a new interpretation of the "significance of the city in American history."[25]

1

ℳ

The Spirit of the Times: Ideology

If there be one half century in the history of any people, upon which
the mind may dwell, with scarcely a wish that it had been different,
such I regard the first half century of our history.

—TIMOTHY WALKER, 1838

The Semi-Centennial Celebration

On the day after Christmas, December 26, 1838, Cincinnati celebrated
its fiftieth anniversary. At sunrise a salvo of thirteen guns, one for each of
the original states of the Union, broke the clear, cold morning air and
ushered in the Semi-Centennial Day festivities. Later in the morning a
grand procession formed along Walnut Street. At the head of the line
stood four militia companies, followed by several bands of music, a group
of distinguished old pioneers, the city officials, the celebration committee, and a number of solid citizens bringing up the rear. The procession
first headed south toward the river, but at Front Street it turned east one
block to Main Street, where it then turned north and marched three
blocks up the hill to the First Presbyterian Church. The old church was
already crowded with women and children dressed in their holiday best,
but the members of the procession made their way in, filling every corner
of the building and overflowing into the narrow aisles. The gathering
then settled down to hear the opening ceremonies and the main feature of
the day, the anniversary oration.

The orator for the honored occasion was Daniel Drake, local physician,
writer, teacher, and community leader, an old pioneer who had arrived in
Cincinnati at the beginning of the century and had been a guiding spirit
in the city's development ever since. As much as any man present at the

celebration, Dr. Drake epitomized the achievement of his beloved city. When Drake rose to take the podium, a shudder ran through the crowd, an instinctive response to the tremendous pile of manuscript in his hand. The good doctor immediately assured his audience that they were free to leave whenever they became fatigued, and then launched into his topic, the growth and progress of Cincinnati. Step-by-step the orator spun out the story of the city's rise out of the frontier wilderness and flowering into the "Queen of the West." For three and a half hours Drake reviewed the familiar story, in infinite detail, and with many interesting anecdotes. Finally, in midafternoon, the extended discourse, which one reviewer called "a perfect mastodon," lumbered to a close.

As the assembled citizens spilled out of the church, some of them headed to the Pearl Street House, where the city fathers, the old pioneers, and nearly two hundred other distinguished citizens sat down to a public dinner. Presiding over the affair was Nathan Guilford, a prominent law-yer and merchant, sponsor of many educational and cultural activities in the community, and a supporter of all good causes. Like Dr. Drake, Nathan Guilford was one of the men who had built Cincinnati and he, too, was a choice representative of the best of its citizens. The public dinner, like the anniversary oration, was designed on a grand scale. The diners had their choice of meat, poultry, game, and oysters, many kinds of vegetables, puddings, pies, jellies, fruits, and nuts, all washed down with gallons of champagne, sherry, and Madeira. After eating their fill of this "sumptuous and elegant meal," the gentlemen settled back in their chairs and drank the evening away with unnumbered toasts to the past, present, and future. At nightfall a twenty-six gun salute, one for each of the present states of the Union, punctuated their reverie and marked the grand finale of the Semi-Centennial Celebration.

Later that night, as Cincinnatians made their way through the dark streets to their homes, they might well have reflected that the day's festiv-ities were a fitting tribute to their remarkable accomplishments. The Semi-Centennial Celebration commemorated an "extraordinary revolu-tion," one resident wrote, the transformation in the short span of fifty years of a "perfect wilderness, inhabited alone by savages and wild beasts," into a community of nearly fifty thousand souls, the largest city in the West, and a metropolis which "vies with any of its Atlantic contempo-raries in the elegance of its buildings, the refinement of its manners, the luxuries of its living, and the intelligence and enterprise of its citizens."[1]

Shared Advantages and Aspirations

Hyperbole and other excesses are the standard fare of anniversaries. But the grandiose proportions and grandiloquent rhetoric of the Cincinnati Semi-Centennial Celebration were characteristic of the general spirit in the city at the time. There was a pervasive feeling in the community of pride in past accomplishments and confidence in continued progress and prosperity. There was a sense of community identity, based on shared experiences and expectations, that seemed to infuse and unite most, if not all, Cincinnatians.

The basis of this community identity was a stylized account of the short but spectacular history of the city. The story usually went something like this: Cincinnati had grown from a small frontier outpost, huddled along the Ohio River bank and surrounded by hostile Indians, to become a modest, prosperous village serving the early nineteenth-century migrants who passed through on their way west. With the development of river and canal commerce in the 1820s and 1830s, Cincinnati emerged as the most prominent and diversified metropolis west of the Allegheny Mountains. The original settlement of several hundred hearty pioneers had grown into a community of nearly fifty thousand souls and had spread out from the confines of the old Fort Washington to a distance of more than a mile in radius. As Cincinnati grew, the economy diversified, with pork-packing houses and ship-building shops to complement the earlier grain mills and mercantile houses. At the same time there was a proliferation of public and private institutions that offered most of the opportunities for good works, self-improvement, and entertainment of which eastern cities boasted.

During the short span of fifty years Cincinnatians had suffered through flood, fire, and pestilence, just as they had survived economic depression, political division, and inter-urban competition. First the city had passed Lexington and Louisville, then it had overcome the challenge of Pittsburgh, and it had kept on growing and prospering, at an ever-increasing rate, so that there seemed to be no end in sight. Most remarkable of all, this had occurred within the lifetime of men who were still alive and active in the community.

Most Cincinnatians were less interested in the details of the city's dramatic development than in its general significance and future implications. What, they asked, were the particular advantages of the

Queen City and what were its aspirations for the future? During the 1830s and 1840s answers to these questions filled the pages of local newspapers and guidebooks, they appeared in private letters and diaries, and they often served as the theme of public speeches by community leaders. Foreigners asked the same questions when they visited Cincinnati, and many of their travel accounts reported the answers and impressions they received.[2]

By 1840 the answers to these questions had been repeated over and over and refined into a coherent argument about Cincinnati's past achievements, present character, and future prospects. Cincinnati was, first and foremost, blessed with a strategic location and a beautiful setting. Second, the city had developed a diversified, stable economy and a full ensemble of educational and religious institutions. Third, it was a harmonious, happy community with a strong sense of social order and civic responsibility. Finally, as a result of these fortuitous local conditions, and the larger pattern of national development, Cincinnati enjoyed the happy prospect of ever-increasing progress and permanent prosperity.[3]

This argument was developed by a small group of local leaders, but it was clearly designed to express the general attitudes of the larger community. It drew on the common elements of their personal experience and expectations, defined the unique advantages of their city and the general values and goals which united them, and served to initiate newcomers to the community and instill a greater sense of commitment among the established residents.

Part fact, part fancy, this argument had become, by the time of the Semi-Centennial Celebration, an integral part of the civic consciousness of most, if not all, Cincinnatians. If some members of the community questioned or rejected the argument, they had not yet made their objections known to the public or developed an alternative argument. While certain elements in the accepted argument were erroneous or exaggerated, constant repetition in statements by local leaders and in travel accounts from the outside gave it a general aura of authority.

A Strategic Location

Cincinnati's first and foremost advantage, local boosters and foreign travelers agreed, was its strategic location on the Ohio River. Situated on the northern bank of "La Belle Rivière," as residents affectionately called her, across from the mouth of the Licking River, the pioneer village immediately became an important way station and provisioning center for the wave of western migrants in the early nineteenth century. The pioneers came through the Cumberland Road, changed to flatboats at Pittsburgh, and floated down the Ohio River to Cincinnati, where they fanned out northward into the rich country of the Miami Valley or prepared themselves to tackle the frontier farther west.

With the triumph of the steamboat on the western rivers in the 1820s, Cincinnati secured its supremacy on the Ohio River by becoming a major boat-building center and the great midway port on the long haul from Pittsburgh to New Orleans. The river was, indeed, the lifeline of the Cincinnati economy during this period. Every spring and fall as many as fifty steamers stood side-by-side along the riverfront quay, loading and unloading cargoes, which local merchants sold at handsome profits. No less important were the profits that East End shipbuilders made from the sale of more than thirty boats yearly. It was only fitting that a Cincinnatian pronounced, "The name of Fulton should be cherished here with that of Washington: if the one conducted us to liberty, the other has given us prosperity—if the one broke the chains that bound us to a foreign country, the other has extended the channels of intercourse, and multiplied the ties which bind us to each other." During the 1830s and 1840s, as more and more high-stacked, triple-decked steamers crowded along the Cincinnati waterfront, most residents believed that the reign of the Ohio River steamboat would continue indefinitely, and with it the city's burgeoning fortunes.[4]

As the city grew, and the surrounding countryside was settled, Cincinnatians came to appreciate a second, supplementary advantage of their physical situation. They "seemed to be," as one resident wrote later, in the middle of "land flowing with milk and honey." The fertile Miami Valley, to the north and west of the city, was an immensely rich natural breadbasket where, during the late summer months, the undulating fields of grain spread across the horizon "tall enough to cover a man on horseback" and "green as a bank of moss." The price of land was so low and wages for labor so high that in the early years a man could purchase an acre of land with a day's work. With cultivation of the land surrounding the city, Cincinnatians reaped the harvest, literally, of the farmers who carried their grain and livestock to the city's mills and slaughterhouses. Meatpacking was Cincinnati's leading industry by the 1830s, and the reason for the infamous sobriquet "Porkopolis."[5]

In order to secure the flow of grain and pigs from its bountiful hinterland, Cincinnati pushed through the construction of the Miami Canal. In the late 1820s and early 1830s, after it had reached Dayton and then the area of central Ohio, the Miami Canal proved to be an enormously profitable feeder swelling the Queen City's commerce. Cincinnati reached out in other directions, too, with turnpikes to siphon off the rich resources of the entire Ohio Valley. During the 1830s Cincinnatians showed considerable foresight and expended large sums of money in promoting internal improvements to complement their river trade. A review of this transportation network described the achievements as well as the ambitions of the Cincinnati promoters:

> A canal already connects the interior with Cincinnati, and in a few years, beyond a doubt, the whole region from that city to Lake Erie will be traversed by a canal and a railroad; while in Cincinnati, as a centre, will radiate, in addition to these, a most admirable McAdamized turnpike-road . . . "a canal and a railroad" to Indiana; three other McAdamized turnpikes, already constructed in part, two to meet the National Road in Ohio, the third to reach the centre of Kentucky, Tennessee, and South Carolina, with branches to North Carolina and Georgia, is to rival the Mississippi, and make the West and the South one, as the West and the Southwest are already one.

Needless to say, Cincinnati would be the hub of this new transportation system—the "Western Emporium" for all of the trade in the "*North American Valley.*"[6]

At this time Cincinnatians assumed that their central location in the Ohio Valley, dominating the river trade and controlling the network of internal canals and roads, assured their continued growth and prosperity. Strategically located in the heart of a vast three-state area, from the Great Lakes to Tennessee and from the Alleghenies to the Mississippi River, Cincinnati stood at the center of the richest inland empire of agricultural and mineral wealth in the United States. After reviewing this situation, a local guidebook concluded:

> The region thus connected by this system of public works, embraces within its bounds at least half a million people, and must speedily quadruple that number, and may easily sustain eight millions of people with-

out being excessively populous. It is by contemplating this fact, in connection with the vast *internal commerce,* arising from the wants and industry of such a people . . . that we can adequately comprehend the rapid and permanent growth of Cincinnati.[7]

A Beautiful City

Just as Cincinnatians exploited their strategic location and developed the major entrepôt of the Ohio Valley, so they took advantage of their physical setting and built a remarkably beautiful city. In the winter of 1788, when the original settlers floated down the Ohio River in search of a new home, they passed many sites that would have been suitable for their small party. But they waited until they came to a wide break in the hilly wooded river banks, where a long level plain spread out, surrounded by high-rising hills on three sides. Here, in a corner of this natural amphitheater, the founders stopped, and built the first crude huts that were the basis for the future metropolis.[8]

Along the river's edge was a marshy beach bottom spotted with an assortment of sycamore, cottonwoods, and water maples and inhabited by raccoons and opossums. This low-lying riverfront area extended approximately eight hundred feet to the north, where a short but very steep slope marked the line of a higher, dryer plateau where beech, yellow poplar, and hickory trees receded into the distance. Along the eastern and western fringes of this second plateau, two shallow creeks meandered until they emptied into the Ohio River. To the east, north, and west rose seven hills, with an average height of three hundred feet, in a semicircular arc that enclosed the natural amphitheater for twelve miles in circumference. It was, everyone agreed, an ideal setting for a great city and large enough for Cincinnati to grow indefinitely.

For travelers coming down the Ohio River in the 1830s the appearance of Cincinnati was a thrilling sight. After passing miles and miles of thickly wooded shores and clay bluffs rising two to three hundred feet above the river's edge, with only an occasional cabin or small village to break the monopoly of endless wilderness, it seemed like an apparition to see a large city, with homes, churches, warehouses, and factories, spread out before their eyes. The public landing, which extended a thousand feet along the riverfront and covered an area of ten acres, was the heart of the city's business activity. Behind, on the north side of Front Street, stood the warehouses, stores, and ships that transacted most of the river trade. To the east, along lower Broadway, were many of the important public buildings, banks, and hotels. To the north, along Broadway and on the brow of the second terrace, which was Fourth Street, stood many of Cincinnati's finest residences. Upriver, along the Miami Canal east of the city, were many of the city's large foundries, ship-building yards, and packinghouses. To the west, beyond Western Row, lay the Mill Creek meadows and a few scattered brick and lumber yards.[9]

For the first forty years Cincinnati grew within the confines of the long lower plateau called "the Bottom." It was not until the 1830s that residents ascended the second plateau, called "the Hill," to take advantage of the healthier climate and the commanding view. In 1840, however, much activity was still concentrated in the Bottom, where the mass of square one-, two-, and three-story buildings was broken only by the streets which ran at regular intervals north–south and east–west. The Miami Canal, which flowed into the city from the northwest, cut east across the city a mile north of the river and then ran south along the Deer Creek into the Ohio River, marking the limits of population concentration in the city. Although some visitors complained about the want of design in the city's appearance and the lack of open spaces or parks, most marveled at the sight of a "real city," comparable to those they had seen in the East, springing up in the midst of the western wilderness.

Although nearly fifty thousand people were living in the city in 1840, Cincinnati still had the appearance of an overgrown town rather than a large modern city. Nearly everyone lived within a concentrated mile-square area and could easily walk to the places where they worked and shopped. There were few horses or carriages used within the city, and no public transportation. The three market houses were centrally located in different parts of the city, and small retail stores and artisan shops were distributed throughout the settled area. Cincinnatians often complained about the muddy, rutted street surfaces and the lack of any lighting at night, but they generally seemed to enjoy living within a small, densely populated, multipurpose "walking city."[10]

At this time, Cincinnati was remarkably free from the soot and smoke that marred the appearance of most large industrial cities: much of the work in the Queen City, such as shoe and clothing manufacturing, was done by hand in the "upper stories, or in the rear shops of the warehouses, out of sight." The large foundries and ship-building shops were concentrated along the river and canal southeast of the city in the Flatiron District, which was run by water power and steam engines rather than by noxious coal-burning furnaces. And the notorious slaughterhouses, where the screams and stench of the victims pierced the air, and from which a steady stream of blood and gore ran into the Deer Creek, were located a good distance east of the main residential and business sections of the city.[11]

It was a "beautiful city," wrote Charles Dickens after his visit in 1842. This caustic critic was "quite charmed" by the city with its "clean houses of red and white, its well-paved roads and footways of bright tile." At this time the city had a remarkably clear and fresh appearance, since many of the brick and frame buildings were less than ten years old. Although the city had its architectural abortions, notably Mrs. Trollope's Bazaar, most visitors were pleased with the variety of the architecture and the design of the city. Dickens declared the "invention and fancy in the varying styles" of buildings to be "perfectly delightful" and commended the city for its "broad and airy streets," the "elegance and neatness" of its residences, and its "refreshing and agreeable" gardens. Looking down on the city from Mount Auburn, north of the city, the noted English author surveyed the entire city spread out below. It was, he concluded, "a picture of remarkable beauty."[12]

A Diversified and Stable Economy

During the 1830s Cincinnati enjoyed almost uninterrupted prosperity as local enterprise developed a diversified and stable economic system. Riding the wave of increased western settlement, which provided a demand for goods and a supply of foodstuffs, Cincinnati was less affected than eastern cities by economic crises such as the Jackson bank veto and the Panic of 1837, and all sectors of the local economy made substantial advances during this decade. Despite particular difficulties and the periodic fears of some, this was a time, an editor asserted, when "the only change which has occurred . . . is the gradual one from poverty to comparative wealth . . . that goes on unchecked; never . . . was there a period of greater abundance in all the advantages and facilities of successful industry than what now prevails." In the winter of 1840–41, and again in 1841–42, Cincinnati suffered a short economic relapse due primarily to the frozen river trade and curtailment of building in the cold weather.

But throughout this period the local economy continued to grow, and many shared in the general progress and prosperity.[13]

In 1840 the foundation of the local economy continued to be the provisioning of migrants and new settlers, who purchased many of the staples and household utensils necessary for their new homes. However, Cincinnatians soon began to produce more of the goods they sold. Instead of buying all of their merchandise in the East, from Philadelphia and New York manufacturers, and confining themselves to middleman profits, enterprising local merchants began to make the furniture, farm implements, clothing, saddles, pottery, and paper that they sold to new settlers and to the peddlers and small-town dealers who distributed these goods throughout the hinterland. Thus Cincinnatians profited doubly as the local economy swelled with both mercantile and manufacturing revenue.

In 1840 commerce was the leading sector of the Cincinnati economy. According to Charles Cist, who took the federal census in the city, there was more than $18 million invested in local mercantile houses—$5,200,000 in wholesale businesses, $12,877,000 in retail stores. The city imported more than $11 million of foodstuffs—principally flour, whiskey, corn, beef, pork, and lard—and exported an estimated $9 million in processed foods and manufactures. The large mercantile emporiums along Front and Pearl Streets—the clearinghouses and warehouses of the local merchant princes—were the scene of daily transactions that contributed a major share to Cincinnati's prosperity.[14]

During the 1830s industry had developed so "silently and gradually" in Cincinnati, a local authority remarked, that "few, even of our own citizens, are aware of the extent and importance of manufacturing interest." In 1840 there were 1,594 different establishments employing 10,608 men and producing goods worth $17,328,651. This second sector of the local economy was a source of special satisfaction to Cincinnatians, since it decreased their dependence on the East and helped to balance the general economy.

Although there was some difference of opinion as to the quality of the local products—Cincinnati boosters described them as being of "superior quality," while Michael Chevalier, a visitor from France, indicated that they were of no more than "ordinary quality"—there was general agreement that the city possessed a wide variety of competent mechanics and a sufficient amount of technical knowledge and experience to challenge the industrial centers of the East. The 1838 exhibition of local products at the Ohio Mechanics Institute included everything from carriages to corsets, saddles to scientific instruments, books to boilers, and prize hams to delicate harmonicas, and marked the formal opening of an industrial challenge that would catapult Cincinnati into third place as a manufacturing center of the United States at midcentury.[15]

Property investment was the third sector of the Cincinnati economy in 1840. Since the founding of the city, property speculation was a popular and often profitable form of investment, and the wealth of many of the early leaders of the community was based largely on the increased value of their real estate holdings. The high risk of commercial ventures, the failure of the United States Bank in 1819, and the need for mechanical skill or large amounts of money to enter manufacturing led many to invest their extra capital in property and watch its value increase with the growth of the city. The profits of land speculators "defy any parallel," one enthusiastic local booster exclaimed, "except what may be found in the legend of Aladdin and his wonderful lamp." There was, for example, the lot on the corner of Main and Front Street, which had cost the original owner exactly $2.00 in 1789. In 1840 there were thirteen stores on the property, which paid an estimated rent of $14,250. This meant, Cist noted, that by a conservative evaluation the land was now worth $237,000, or that the property had doubled in value every three years. Such increases in property values explain why many accepted as a rule of thumb that *"the ground alone is worth more than it is with the buildings added to it."*[16]

The entire Cincinnati economy rested upon a local banking system that, in 1840, seemed to be firmly established and secure. In the early days of the city, banks had lacked specie and had been overly optimistic in their speculation. The failure of the first United States Bank in 1819 had ruined some of the leading members of the community and retarded the local economy for several years. But in the 1830s the state legislature chartered a number of new banks that were able to weather the Panic of 1837. Even though the amount of their working capital was severely reduced, there were no failures, and most faced the future with renewed confidence in the stability and sobriety of their economic system. As a report in 1841 proclaimed, "The fact that this immense amount ($3,276,193) was deducted in one year from the business capital of the city, without producing bankruptcies . . . forms conclusive proof that our money operations were based on a sound and healthy business, and that our mechanics and merchants sustain a high commercial character."[17]

A thorough review of the Cincinnati economy in a period of national economic depression, this report pointed to three critical factors. First was a diversification of the economy: "The three great interests of manufacturing, commerce, and the produce business divide the wealth and industry of our citizens; it seldom happens that all interests are paralyzed at the same time, and when one of them is depressed, there is usually a sustaining power in the others." Second, Cincinnati produced a wide variety of essential articles for which there was a steady demand. As Michael Chevalier had observed years earlier, "The prosperity of Cincinnati rests upon the sure basis of the prosperity of the west, upon the supply of articles of the first necessity of the bulk of the community." Finally, there was a general diffusion of wealth throughout the entire population, which protected the community from disaster caused by a few failures and provided a strong and steady market for local goods: "Our active business capital is distributed into many hands. Instead of having a few heavy capitalists, we have a great number of persons of moderate means. The temptation to imprudent speculation, as well as to extravagant living, is modified by the distribution of wealth; and as a general rule our capital is active, and employed in fair business operations." Cincinnatians attributed their general economic progress and prosperity during the late 1830s to these particular local conditions. "The rapid growth of Cincinnati during a period of general financial embarrassment and of much commercial depression" provided, a local newspaper declared in 1840, "the highest evidence that the foundations of her prosperity are laid deep and strong."[18]

Institutions and the Social Order

In 1841 a group of prominent men tried to persuade Congress to establish a national armory in the Queen City. It would bring new people and prosperity to the city and provide an official sanction to Cincinnati's claim as the Colossus of the West. To promote the cause, local leaders published a pamphlet describing the city and its many advantages. After enumerating the advantages of the city's strategic location, its beautiful situation, and its position as the financial, commercial, and manufacturing center of the west, the argument turned to "the advantages of society, or of the means of education and religious instruction." It was the fact that Cincinnati had "in complete operation, all the institutions of social order," the promoters claimed, that attracted the "continual influx of a valuable population" and then "elevated them to their proper standing in society."[19]

Educational and religious institutions were considered to be of particular importance because they benefited the individuals in the community and helped to mold them into a harmonious, happy society. Schools provided the instruction necessary for individuals to become self-sufficient, contributing members of the society. Churches satisfied their spiritual needs and encouraged a sense of moral order. The influence of these institutions was suggested in David Shaffer's *Cincinnati Directory for 1840:*

> In truth, when we consider the fact that, in a perfectly democratic state of society, where no strong police exists, and no military force at all is present,—breaches of order are rare and decreasing; that Free Schools have been founded by the popular will; that churches are yearly rising, and that all moves on in comparative harmony,—we may well feel assured that democracy and true Christian equality are, what our fathers believed them to be, the cornerstone of quiet and happiness.

Schools and churches socialized members of the community and instilled the "good morals" and "orderly habits" of which local boosters boasted.[20]

It was generally agreed that the progress of morality and Christianity in Cincinnati was no less spectacular than that of the city's population and economy. Soon after the first settlers arrived, they organized a church. In January 1792—after several years of informal meetings in private homes—over a hundred men signed a subscription list, pledging to help pay for the building of the First Presbyterian Church. By 1819, when the local population was nearly ten thousand, there were ten houses of worship, one with an estimated seven hundred communicants. During the next two decades over thirty new churches were established in the community, representing many different denominations; and by 1840 Shaffer boasted that "the number of churches is greater, in proportion to the [number of] inhabitants, than any city in the United States."[21]

The beneficial effects of religion were evident to one visitor to the Queen City in the summer of 1840, who concluded, after a thorough survey of the churches of the community, that "the state of religion and morals in this place are such as would please every lover of Jesus and of good order." Another visitor, the well-known English traveler James S. Buckingham, also praised Cincinnati for its high state of morality and found at least two-thirds of the residents affiliated, in some way, with one of the many religious denominations in the community. The popularity of prominent ministers and the large attendance at their sermons, the progress of temperance reform in the community, and the lack of support for theaters and other places of vice were generally cited as evidence of the strong religious character of Cincinnatians.[22]

Education was the other important area to which Cincinnati's civic leaders turned first in the establishment of local institutions. The first log schoolhouse opened in 1792; by 1800 a private school offered a full curriculum including Latin, Greek, navigation, astronomy, and rhetoric; and in 1815 the city fathers chartered a Lancasterian school. During the next twenty-five years the addition of a variety of evening schools, private academies, colleges, and professional schools gave the city the reputation of the "Athens of the West." More important, as a result of efforts by Cincinnatians like Nathan Guilford in the 1820s, Ohio instituted free public schools. According to one local booster, there were nearly seven thousand students in the city by 1840: four hundred in local colleges, fifteen hundred in academies, and five thousand in the common schools.[23]

Education was vigorously supported by Cincinnatians not only for its utilitarian value but also because it helped to socialize the new members of society. Along with the basic skills, public schools provided students with training in proper conduct and respect for law and order. Similarly, the Ohio Mechanics Institute lectures discussed the subjects of religion, morality, and the responsibilities of citizenship as often as the more mundane matters of technical innovations and ways in which to improve one's vocational skills. The public schools, Sunday schools, and the various libraries and institutes for workingmen and immigrant groups, therefore, all played an important role in the process of community indoctrination. As Rev. Benjamin P. Aydelotte, president of Woodward College and one of the religious and educational leaders of the community wrote, such institutions "best prepare us for *our peculiar duties as citizens of a free country.*"[24]

Cincinnati's schools and churches were generally considered to be the most important social institutions in the community because they had played a central role in the development of the city, they affected the largest proportion of its population, and they had the greatest influence on its character. In describing the role of religious and educational institutions in the community, local boosters tended to disregard doctrinal and social differences and emphasized instead the general values of Christian virtue and moral order that they all promoted. The general significance of these social institutions was that they shared a concern for moral character and social harmony and were instrumental in instilling these values in the members of the community.

Politics and Civic Responsibility

Just as the basic values of the community were instilled by the local schools and churches so were they manifest through local politics. During the five-year period 1837–42 a number of local issues came up in Cincinnati elections concerning the future development of the city, the proper role of the municipal government, and its responsibility in enforcing moral order. An examination of these issues—the manner in which they were defined, discussed, and decided—can help to clarify the underlying assumptions of the community and the degree to which the citizens accepted and acted upon them. The evidence suggests that there was a strong impetus to expand the role of local government in economic and social affairs and that most Cincinnati voters agreed to, or accepted, this philosophy of civic responsibility.

Between 1837 and 1842 Cincinnatians faced five different issues which turned on the question of the proper role of local government: municipal assistance for internal improvements, public ownership of the Waterworks, the right of the city to tax farmers selling their produce in local markets, reform of the city charter to limit the power of elected officials, and the restriction of licensing of coffeehouses. Each of these issues was defined largely in terms of the future development of the city. The particular decisions of whether to increase the responsibilities of the municipal government depended fundamentally on the degree to which the voters agreed with local boosters that economic progress should be promoted and the prevailing order maintained. While the number of citizens who voted in these elections was small, the size of the majority in each case was substantial; this suggests that although the level of community interest in these issues may have been low, the degree of agreement among the voters was considerable.

Cincinnatians voted for several large loans of municipal funds to support internal improvements. The issue under consideration was not only whether the city should encourage the building of canals and railroads but, more important, whether the municipal tax revenue should be used to help finance these projects. In 1837 Cincinnati voters agreed that the city should allocate $600,000 for the completion of the Little Miami Railroad and the Whitewater Canal and the building of the proposed Charleston–Cincinnati Railroad. When the latter project fell through, voters later agreed to transfer the $200,000 granted to the railroad to the Whitewater Canal. When the Canal ran into more difficulties in 1841, the city put another $200,000 into the enterprise. Thus, in a five-year period marked by national depression Cincinnatians voted to spend $800,000 of their tax money to promote progress and prosperity in the city.[25]

After fifteen years of steadfast opposition to the idea, Cincinnati voters finally agreed to buy the Cincinnati Waterworks in 1839. Built in 1824 by a group of prominent local businessmen who hoped to turn it over to the city with some compensation for their efforts, the Waterworks immediately became a symbol of potential municipal intrusion into private enterprise and the unjustified expansion of civic responsibility. Despite constant complaints about the company's services and charges, the local electorate rejected four different offers in the early 1830s to sell the Waterworks to the city. Then, in 1838, in a heated campaign marked by several sensational stories suggesting that the company was polluting their water, the voters agreed to purchase the Waterworks for $300,000, or fifteen times the price at which it was originally offered. This election marked a decisive turnabout in local governmental powers and the beginning of the expansion of municipal services, such as the paid fire department and police force, in the years that followed.[26]

At the beginning of 1840 another issue, the "Market Wagon War," aroused public opinion about the rights and responsibilities of outsiders using the city's facilities. Farmers from around Cincinnati often brought their produce to the local markets and sold it from the backs of their wagons. In 1839 the city council voted to impose a small tax "as compensation for the injuries inflicted on the pavements by the stamping of horses, and in remuneration for the expense of removing the filth they deposited." The state courts, controlled by Democrats who had a strong attachment to the rural electorate, declared the tax unlawful. But in the 1840 spring elections, which turned largely on this issue, local voters turned out all of the men who had opposed the tax and elected men who promised to enforce it, in defiance of the ruling of the state court.[27]

The 1840 municipal election also indicated that the majority of Cincinnati voters were satisfied with the existing form of municipal government, one which gave broad powers to a city council dominated by a small group of local leaders. Early in the year a revision of the city charter was proposed that would have limited the authority and privileges of the city council by prohibiting members from holding any outside position where they might profit from work done for the city, and by making all civic officers elective rather than appointive. The stated purpose of the reform was to allow the citizens to have a greater control over the selection of their constables, watchmen, and inspectors, and to end the alleged corruption in government contracts. But the opponents of the charter revision, who posed as "Good Order Men," argued that this was an attempt to undermine the laws and turn the government over to the "disreputable" elements in society. Cincinnati voters turned down the proposed revision by an overwhelming majority, apparently agreeing with "An Aged Citizen," who maintained that the present government was adequate and effective, that the councilmen acted in the best interests of the entire community, and that the election of civic officers would produce local dissension and strife. The "Good Order" victory in April 1840 suggested that a confident, corporate concept of government prevailed at this time and that Cincinnati voters were willing to delegate to their elected officials broad powers over local affairs.[28]

These powers extended, for a time at least, to the control of alcoholic consumption, which many local leaders saw as a threat to community order. In 1838 citizens voted into office a group of new councilmen who promised to curb the licensing of "coffeehouses" and to try to stop the spread of intemperance and other vice in the city. This reform effort coincided with a general temperance crusade led by the churches during the late 1830s and supported by many of the leading members of the community. The ostensible purpose was to combat the evils of liquor, but an underlying motive may well have been fear of possible "excesses" of the yet "uncivilized" German immigrants, who were arriving in increasing numbers and brought with them a strong liking for beer.

It was soon clear, however, that this kind of legislation could not curtail established drinking habits and that the actual effect was to benefit the licensed coffeehouse owners. Further, municipal efforts to control the sale of liquor were widely interpreted as being discriminatory to Germans and had the effect of antagonizing the newcomers and alienating them from their local government. For a year or so, city council attempted to stop the flow of liquor—refusing to sell any new licenses or to renew old ones—and then recognized the futility and divisiveness of their efforts and then gave up. In 1841 the former temperance councilmen were decisively defeated. From this point on, there were no more attempts to use municipal government to legislate social behavior. This short but ambitious exercise in social improvement and control was abandoned in the name of personal freedom and community harmony.[29]

Throughout this five-year period local politics was dominated by the discussion and decision of these issues. Candidates for local offices generally ran as individuals, on their personal reputations and positions on specific issues. The local Whig and Democratic party organizations did not run their own slates of candidates and generally did not intrude into municipal elections. The local press devoted little editorial space or energy to these elections beyond printing the names of the candidates and stating their own preferences. The electorate demonstrated relatively little interest in their outcome, voting in municipal elections in less than half the strength that they did in state or national elections. But the outcome of these elections was always decisive, with a majority of at least 70% on every issue and, with one exception, all seven city wards always supporting the majority decision.

Despite the general lack of community interest and involvement in these local elections, most Cincinnati voters seemed to agree with, or accept, the idea that municipal government should take a strong, active role in the development of the city. The high degree of consensus manifest in these five particular decisions suggests that there was an underlying consensus in the community that economic progress should be promoted and social harmony, even at the cost of moral improvement, had to be secured. Cincinnatians seemed to be content to be led by a small group of prominent citizens who defined what was in the best interests of the community, and gave them broad powers to direct local development. This general pattern of consensus in local politics around 1840 reflected a more general confident, corporate concept of society.[30]

The Fabric of Community Identity

The spirit of boosterism was prevalent in American boomtowns just as the sense of boundlessness was pervasive in the Jacksonian period. The literature arguing Cincinnati's particular advantages and aspirations drew on many of the themes of opportunity and optimism that were common in the booster mentality and Jacksonian rhetoric. But the focus of the argument was clearly local, stressing the special qualities that were unique to the city and that united its citizens. Its purpose was to define the specific world in which Cincinnatians lived and the common values and goals that they shared. It articulated, in a larger context, the ideology of "community-ism" through which Cincinnati boosters attempted to instill a particular sense of corporate identity and civic consciousness.[31]

In this booster literature, therefore, Cincinnati represented a state of mind as much as a geographical location. Local spokesmen and foreign observers described the city not only in terms of its actual location, size, and development but also, and more important, in terms of its inherent assets, character, and destiny. The stylized story of the short but spectacular history of the city revealed, according to one orator, a "magical agency" that seemed to be guiding the Queen City. Descriptions of Cincinnati's situation, appearance, economy, institutions, and politics implied that there was some inevitable, natural process at work in the development of the city. Defined in this way, Cincinnati took on an organic character, with a strong and distinctive corporate identity.[32]

This sense of community identity was drawn out of the common experience and expectations of Cincinnatians and woven by local boosters into a coherent pattern that was, they contended, the true representation of Cincinnati. The many different natural advantages of the city's strategic location and beautiful situation can be described as the particular threads forming the warp of the fabric. And each of the developments in the city's economy and institutions can be described as the distinctive threads forming the woof of the fabric. The natural advantages and man-made achievements complemented one another and brought out the general pattern in the fabric. This pattern, as interpreted by local boosters, portrayed a happy, harmonious community destined to enjoy ever-increasing progress and permanent prosperity.

This concept of community served as a kind of security blanket for Cincinnati at this time. It drew the individuals in the community together and, through a sense of common attachment, instilled a stronger feeling of unity and purpose. It supported them through personal disappointments and petty differences and, through a sense of shared enterprise, reinforced a general spirit of cooperation and confidence. It sustained the essential optimism of the community and, by providing a sense of special destiny, generated new and greater hopes for the future. Bound together in this manner, Cincinnatians came to see themselves as an integral part of the ongoing success of the city.

Public occasions such as the Cincinnati Semi-Centennial Day Celebration provided an opportunity for members of the community to come together to review their shared experiences and renew their sense of common identity. In the original call for a formal celebration of Cincinnati's fiftieth anniversary, Edward D. Mansfield, editor of the influential Cincinnati *Chronicle,* made this purpose clear: "All sects, political and religious, all casts [*sic*] and classes, all ages, both sexes, and emigrants not less than natives, should put forth their representatives and unite in a common anthem of patriotism. Then we should be brought into sympathy with each other; and becoming united in recollections, press forward in the development of those noble destinies, which cannot be contemplated without rapture." Mansfield's editorial is significant not only in its explicit statement of the integrative function of such public celebrations but also in its implicit suggestion of the necessity of including all of the many different elements within the community on these occasions.[33]

In fact, not all Cincinnatians attended the Semi-Centennial Day Celebration, nor did they all adhere to the community ideology. These public occasions were dominated by the older and more prominent members of the community; the booster literature was developed by a small group of native, articulate promoters; civic institutions were directed by a coterie of established, successful citizens; and local political issues were decided by a minority of the voting population. Despite the differential levels of individual interest and involvement, the community ideology still provided all with some sense of a unique corporate identity.

Beneath the particular arguments describing the special advantages, achievements, and aspirations of the Queen City there was a general underlying assumption that continued progress and prosperity would benefit all. Implicit in the community ideology was a concept of a cohesive corporate community based on an integrated and harmonious social order. In a classic description of this ideal community, Daniel Drake emphasized the importance of consensus and cooperation: "Society has functions to perform which require a harmonious and concerted action at least among its principal members. In every state and in every city, composed of emigrants, it should be the chief political object to introduce and foster a singleness of design and unity of effort, until all shall be ready to cooperate in every project for the common good." Drake's statement is suggestive not only in his definition of the community as a functioning social system but also in his description of the responsibilities of its "emigrants," who must be integrated, and the "principal members," who should provide united leadership.[34]

2

_9_

Character and Composition: Demography

Of the people I can truly say they are a motley crew. We have Germans and Dutch, English and French, Irish and Scotch, Yankees and Buckeyes, and the lordly Virginian and the chivalrous Kentuck . . . all with their peculiar habits. . . . In such a mass of population you will of course expect to find religious denomination as various as the clans of which it is composed and accordingly we have our Catholics and Covenators [*sic*], Campbellites and Dissenters, Reformed Dutch and Low Germans, Episcopalians and Presbyterians, Methodists and Baptists, Swedenbourgians and Quakers, and a host of others the names of which I do not remember.

—ALONZO GARCELON, 1839

Charles Cist and the 1840 Census

In June 1840 Charles Cist began the United States Census of Cincinnati. Every day, for nearly five months, he trudged from door to door, visiting homes, shops, and factories, collecting information on the backgrounds and activities of his fellow citizens. Sometimes, when it was hot, or he met an interesting informant, Cist sat down and listened to stories about the early days of the city and the changes that had occurred in recent years. Cist heard tales of great personal successes and failures, bitter condemnations and lavish praises of the Queen City, and many comments—both shrewd and crackpot—on the character of the community. At the same time Cist formed his own impressions of the city and its people, testing generalizations and noting peculiarities, which made him the outstanding authority on the Cincinnati of his day. By the end of the year Cist had surveyed the entire city—over eight thousand house-

44

holds—recorded and tabulated his data in the large manuscript books that he sent to Washington, and then prepared his material for publication as a popular guidebook, *Cincinnati in 1841.*

While he was taking the census, Cist sent periodic reports of his findings—both statistical and impressionistic—to the local newspapers. These articles, which provided a detailed account of Cincinnati's recent development and present character, were closely followed in the community and widely reprinted abroad. They supplied accurate, authoritative support for the city's claims to spectacular growth and progress. As the ward reports came in, citizens speculated on the final population figure for the city. In 1830 the city had boasted 24,831 residents, better than double the 1820 figure, but few Cincinnatians expected the pattern to continue. Most estimates predicted a population of 40,000, or possibly as high as 45,000. Cist's announcement in November that the official population of Cincinnati was 46,382, therefore, came as a considerable surprise and became the source of renewed community pride and promises of further growth.[1]

After he finished the census, Cist received numerous requests for this material in book form; he collected the census data, the stories he heard, and his own impressions of the city, filled this out with information on the history of the city, its climate, topography, economy, and institutions, and published the guidebook *Cincinnati in 1841.* Similar to D. Drake's and E. D. Mansfield's *Cincinnati in 1826,* and the numerous other guidebooks put out by other cities, Cist's volume was intended to publicize the progress and prosperity of the Queen City and to promote its further growth. Many copies were printed—over four hundred copies were sent to Europe alone—and Cist later looked back with considerable pride on his contribution to Cincinnati during its period of greatest growth.[2]

No less important, the publication of *Cincinnati in 1841* launched Cist on a career as the unofficial booster, chronicler, and statistician of the Queen City in the two decades preceding the Civil War. Born in 1792, the son of a prominent Philadelphia printer, Cist moved west after the War of 1812, worked at an assortment of different jobs in Harmony, Pittsburgh, Zelienople, and Camprun, Pennsylvania, acquired a wife and five children in the process, and then settled down in Cincinnati in 1827. He engaged in various local businesses and became involved in Democratic politics. During the 1830s Cist was a strong supporter of the

Jackson administration and served as a city councilman from the Second Ward for several years. According to newspaper accounts in 1836, when he momentarily lost $100,000 entrusted to him, Cist was an active, responsible, and well-respected member of the Cincinnati community.[3]

In 1840, partly in return for his political services to the party and partly as an effort to assist him during some personal financial difficulties, the Van Buren administration appointed Cist as the official census taker in Cincinnati. Although there were no special qualifications for the job, which was often done in a cursory manner by party retainers, Cist proved to be an unusually capable and conscientious census taker. He had had some experience taking the 1820 census of Harmony, Pennsylvania, and he soon demonstrated a natural talent for surveying and statistical work. Although personally surveying a city of nearly 50,000 residents was long, hot, hard work, Cist evidently enjoyed it and repeated the job every few years, despite the city's burgeoning size.

Following the publication of *Cincinnati in 1841,* Cist compiled and published city directories in 1842 and 1843 and then started his own newspaper, *Cist's Weekly Advertiser.* This four-page weekly, and a short-lived daily edition, offered commercial and financial news, antiquarian stories and documents, and statistical data on population and building developments that Cist collected in his periodic surveys of the city. An indefatigable observer and writer with a clear, easy, and unaffected style, Cist did most of the reporting and writing for the paper himself during its nine-year existence. He also managed to publish some of the newspaper material in book form, in the two-volume *Miscellany,* and brought out new editions to his guidebook, with major revisions, in 1851 and 1859. Then, probably because of old age, and perhaps because of some disillusionment with the city's development in the late 1850s, Cist retired to his farm in College Hill, a neighboring village, where he died in 1868.[4]

The Assumption of Assimilation

In 1840 the Cincinnati population was distinguished by a high degree of vitality, volatility, and variety. An ever-increasing flood of immigrants from the eastern states and abroad during the late 1830s filled the city with a large number of young and ambitious newcomers with diverse backgrounds who were eager to achieve success in the Queen City. Cincinnatians enthusiastically welcomed the newcomers, since immigration was the main source of the city's progress and prosperity, and optimistically assumed that they would integrate themselves into the existing community, adopting the habits, values, and goals of the established leaders. Through indoctrination by local boosters, the socializing influence of the churches and schools, and the beneficial effects of a booming economy, the process of assimilation would assure, it was believed, the orderly expansion of the city.

Immigration was the foundation of Cincinnati's development. The fact that the local population was composed largely of immigrants—men who had the impetus to leave their birthplace, the insight to settle in the Queen City, and the initiative to succeed in their new home—was basic to the formation of the character of the community. Timothy Walker argued that the immigrants were a special, superior breed of men who were the source of the city's strength:

> It may be laid down as an *a priori* truth, that a population made up of immigrants, will contain the hardy and vigorous elements of character, in a far greater proportion, than the same number of persons, born upon the soil, brought up at home, and accustomed to tread in the footsteps of their fathers. As a general rule, it is only the more resolute and energetic class of spirit, that can nerve themselves to the effort required for severing the numerous local, social, and family ties, which bind men to their birthplace. And then, upon arriving in a new country, the very necessity of their condition compels them to think, act, and even originate for themselves. There are no familiar customs, which require only the passive acquiescence of habit. There are no alliances of family or neighborhood, in which one leans upon another, and each helps all. On the contrary, immigrants meet as strangers, unknowing and unknown, and must depend upon their own resources.

Walker characterized the immigrants as strong, self-reliant individualists and claimed that they represented the driving force in the development of Cincinnati.[5]

Cincinnatians welcomed these immigrants in the spirit of "Buckeyeism." As Drake defined it: "Unlike many of its loftier associates, [the Buckeye tree] did not bow its head and wave its arms at a haughty distance, but it might be said to have held out the *right hand of fellowship;* for of all the trees in our forest it is the only one with five leaflets arranged on one stem—an expressive symbol of the human hand." Because the newcomers chose to settle in the Queen City, they enhanced the pride of the community. Because they worked hard and generally prospered, they expanded the local economy. Because they succeeded and often sent enthusiastic reports home, they encouraged further development. The spirit of Buckeyeism asserted that there were unlimited resources and boundless opportunities in the West, and that immigration was the best means for developing this enormous natural potential.[6]

As a result of this large influx of immigrants, Cincinnati was one of the first American large urban melting pots, with a polyglot population that equaled, or exceeded, that of the older eastern centers of New York, Philadelphia, Baltimore, and Boston. Less than 10% of the men in the community had been born in Ohio, Cist reported in *Cincinnati in 1841;* instead, "every state in the Union and almost every part of Europe are represented in the population of this city." Cist had made a special effort to inquire about nativity during his enumeration of the census, and he published the results in his guidebook, listing twenty-seven different states and territories and twenty-five foreign countries from which Cincinnatians were drawn. Similarly, David Shaffer indicated nativity in the personal information listed for each of the householders included in the *Directory for 1840,* making it one of the first and only city directories to provide such information.[7]

Cincinnatians were very conscious of the eclectic composition of the local population, and certain nativity groups came to be characterized in a particular way: the ingenious, indefatigable Yankee, the generous, chivalrous Virginian, the dull, plodding Dutchman. But these differences were generally described by local leaders as a source of special strength and character to the community: "Mixture tends to make man less bigoted," James H. Perkins asserted, "and more catholic in spirit." Many people, no doubt, could not accept this philosophical argument but acted on a more pragmatic basis:

> Necessity compels us to lay aside sectional, political, and religious differences—and to unite as brothers—we are taken away from the local prejudices and accidental influence which at home would have bound us down to one eternal routine of thought and action, and brought into contact with strange beings like ourselves, torn like us from the sphere of early associations; we need their society, their friendship, their confidence, their help, at any rate, we are forced to endure their company—and like reasonable folk, we make the best of it.

This spirit of grudging toleration—based on necessity as well as choice—helps to explain the general harmony that prevailed in Cincinnati in 1840.[8]

There was, however, a more basic reason why Cincinnatians welcomed the immigrants, accepted their difference, and lived together in relative harmony. The underlying assumption about assimilation was that the beneficial climate and conditions of the new western community would dissolve any harmful ingredients in the newcomers' backgrounds and, at the same time, nurture their special strengths and contributions. Calvin Stowe, a recognized authority on the Germans, assured Cincinnatians that these immigrants would not only lose any desire to "set at defiance or undermine existing institutions, or engage in popular commotions" once they had settled down in Cincinnati, but that "their deep and quiet enthusiasm, a speculative tendency, a romance would mingle with and modify our too strong earthiness of disposition, and our too eager pursuit of immediate utility."[9]

By 1840, however, assimilation was more difficult than it had been in the past. During the 1830s the annual rate of population increase jumped from approximately one thousand to nearly four thousand, but many of the newcomers who arrived after 1835 were Germans, with a foreign language and a culture very different from that of the English-speaking majority in the community. During this decade the flood of westward expansion and river trade filled the city with transients, particularly young men, who fueled the local economy but sometimes frustrated the social order. From 1830 to 1840 the local population nearly doubled, from 24,831 to 46,382, but the increased size, complexity, and impersonality of the city made it more difficult to maintain harmony and integration in the community. In 1840 Cincinnati leaders continued to argue, in theory, that assimilation would prevail, but a close examination of the 1840 population suggests that certain basic divisions were in fact emerging within the community.

Priority: The New Settlers and Old Settlers

In the Semi-Centennial Celebration a group of thirty-seven Cincinnatians who had lived in the city for more than thirty years received special recognition. These "old pioneers," as they were affectionately called, had grown up with the city and could attest to its dramatic progress and prosperity. The special affection and attention these old pioneers received may also have been prompted by a sense of their uniqueness. In a community that doubled its population nearly every decade, such a duration of residence was a rare thing. The popularity of stories recounting the city's early history reflected, in part, the fact that many Cincinnatians lacked, but longed for, roots in the city's past. The old pioneers provided a living link between the past and present, a sense of continuity in a period of rapid growth.

During the first half-century of its history, Cincinnati grew in population from 750 in 1800, to 2,540 in 1810, to 9,602 in 1820, to 24,831 in 1830, to 46,382 in 1840. Estimates of the annual rate of growth of the city during this period—based on the number of new buildings erected during the year or the increase in the number of votes cast in local elections—are imprecise, but it appears that the population increased during the 1820s at an average of 1,500 a year, that the annual rate dropped to approximately 1,000 from 1830 through 1835, and that it then accelerated rapidly through 1840, when the population increased by nearly 4,000.[10]

The magnitude of this annual population increase is suggested by a comparison between the *Cincinnati Directory for 1840* and the 1840 Federal Census for Cincinnati. The former enumeration, taken by Shaffer in the late summer of 1839, "compris[ed] the names of householders, heads of families, and those engaged in business." The latter, taken by Cist the following summer, was, according to the official census instructions, a survey of "every *dwelling house*," listing the name of the head of the family and aggregate information on its permanent population. The fact that Cist listed 8,265 heads of census families, while Shaffer listed only 7,494 heads of households, suggests that the number of households in the community was increasing by approximately 10% annually. And the fact that Cist reported the nativity of 12,292 men, while Shaffer reported the nativity for only 10,140, suggests that the total number of men in the city was increasing at nearly double that rate each year.[11]

Since this population growth represents a *net increase*—the annual excess of births over deaths and of in-migrants over out-migrants—the actual number of newcomers who arrived in the city was considerably greater than that suggested by the difference between Cist's and Shaffer's totals. Although the total population steadily increased in the 1830s, there was a high rate of population turnover, with a number of residents leaving the city each year in search of greater opportunities elsewhere. Walker referred to the volatile character of the Cincinnati population in 1830 when he remarked: "Three years make a generation." According to Cist, this high rate of population turnover continued through 1840. In 1843 he reported that he found many men who had left the city temporarily during the late 1830s but returned when they realized that conditions elsewhere were generally worse than they were in Cincinnati. And he referred to the large number of newcomers in the city in 1840 when he noted that this helped to explain why a city with more than thirteen thousand men produced only four thousand votes in the most recent city election. Cist's comments and those of several other contemporary observers indicate that the Cincinnati population in 1840 was highly volatile. This suggests that the actual number of newcomers arriving in the city each year was probably two or three times as great as the net annual population increase.[12]

Of the 13,705 adult white males Cist enumerated in the 1840 census, many were newcomers who arrived in Cincinnati sometime during or after the summer of 1839. It is impossible to determine directly how long these 13,705 men had been residents of Cincinnati in 1840. The census lists only the heads of families by name, and these are often illegible; furthermore, there is no precise occupational or residential information on these heads of families, information necessary for tracing them backward through preceding directories. It is possible, however, to estimate, indirectly, the length of prior residence of the householders listed in the *Directory for 1840,* since the names in it are clearly printed, along with occupational and residential information that can be used to help identify the same person in preceding directories. By tracing every tenth male householder included in the 1840 *Directory* (the Shaffer sample) through the six preceding Cincinnati directories, it is possible to establish the first year in which each is listed. The date of this first directory appearance subtracted from 1840 provides a rough index of "priority," an indirect and imprecise measure of how many years the householder had been an adult resident of the community.[13]

An analysis of the priority of these 868 householders indicates that the majority (56.3%) did not appear in any preceding directory, and had been residents of Cincinnati less than five years. Some of these "new

Table 2.1 Priority of Cincinnati Householders, 1840

Year First Appeared in City Directory	% of Shaffer Sample
1840	56.3
1836	14.2
1834	6.8
1831	6.3
1829	5.8
1825	3.2
1819	7.4
% in town less than 5 years (new settlers)	56.3
% in town between 5 and 10 years	27.3
% in town more than 10 years (old settlers)	16.4

settlers" established themselves in the city quickly and became active, esteemed members of the community. Alphonso Taft arrived in Cincinnati in 1839 and within a year established his place in the legal profession and laid the foundation for a local dynasty. Stephen Molitor arrived in the city in 1837, at the age of thirty-one, took over the *Volksblatt,* a local German-language newspaper, and soon became a pillar in the local German community. But other new settlers had a more difficult time making a place for themselves in Cincinnati and pursued undistinguished careers, or left to search for success in other parts of the country. Augustus Roundy, a young shoemaker from Massachusetts, arrived in 1837, struggled for six years, in the face of constant financial and family difficulties, to establish himself in the Queen City, and then returned home in defeat.[14]

Approximately one-quarter (27.3%) of the householders appear first in the 1831 or 1837 directory and seem to have been adult residents of Cincinnati for five to ten years by 1840. Wilhelm Nast arrived in 1833 as a missionary and soon made a place for himself as the publisher of the *Christliche Apologete* and founder of German Methodism in America. The same year Charles Reemlin arrived from Germany and took a position as clerk in a local grocery store; within a year he became a partner, and in 1837, at the age of twenty-three, bought out his former employer. Flamen Ball came to the city in 1832 as a young man of twenty-three, studied law with several prominent local attorneys, and by 1840 boasted a thriving partnership with Salmon P. Chase. These men all achieved some kind of success soon after arriving in Cincinnati during the 1830s and were still under forty years of age in 1840.[15]

This analysis suggests that more than four-fifths of the householders listed in the *Directory for 1840* had been adult residents of Cincinnati for less than a decade. Most of the householders who arrived in the city sometime during the 1830s did not achieve the rapid or dramatic success that Taft, Molitor, Nast, and Ball did, but the large majority had established themselves in their own homes and had steady jobs by 1840. Some, no doubt, suffered the problems that plagued Augustus Roundy and left the city in subsequent years, but the majority probably prospered and gained some degree of recognition in the community. Over the years they gradually developed friendships and a kind of personal identity; at the same time, they probably developed a certain degree of commitment to Cincinnati.

Less than a fifth (16.4%) of the householders listed in the 1840 *Directory* had been adult residents of Cincinnati for a decade or more. Some of these "old settlers" were still in their thirties in 1840; R. W. Lee, who came to Cincinnati in 1827 to engage in the produce business, was thirty-seven in 1840; and Thomas Yeatman, the son of one of the early settlers of the city, had spent his entire thirty-five years in Cincinnati by 1840. The majority of these old settlers, however, were at least forty years of age in 1840: Bellamy Storer, a prominent local attorney since 1816, was forty-four years old; George C. Miller, who opened the first plow factory in Cincinnati in 1813, was fifty-one; and Jacob Burnet, who started his distinguished career of public service in 1798 as one of the first three judges of the Northwest Territory and authored the first constitution of the State of Ohio, was still, at seventy years old, an active esteemed leader in the community in 1840.[16]

These old settlers, particularly the several hundred men who had been in the community for at least two decades, stood out among the 1840 householders because of their relatively greater maturity and experience. They had been directly involved in the growth of the city over many years and had developed a strong sense of identity as Cincinnatians during this period. By 1840 they had well-established reputations and positions within the community. There were, obviously, important differences and conflicts within this group of old settlers, but there was also a strong sense of familiarity and cohesion that drew them together and gave them a distinctive identity. These men provided much of the leadership in the community and enjoyed a special kind of recognition owing to their greater age, experience, and achievements. It was entirely appropriate that the Semi-Centennial Celebration give special recognition to the old pioneers who had been in the city since 1810.[17]

Nativity: The Yankees, Buckeyes, and Germans

In 1840 Cincinnati was a city of immigrants. The founders of Cincinnati came from New Jersey, and according to Cist, they were soon followed by Pennsylvanians, Virginians, Marylanders, New Yorkers, and New Englanders. Of the foreign-born population, the English and the Scots were the first to arrive, and the Germans the last. By 1840 the adult male population was nearly evenly divided between native-born Americans and emigrants from Europe. Of the 53% who were native-born men, roughly a fifth came from New England, a fifth from New York and New Jersey, a fifth from the border and southern states, a fifth from neighboring Pennsylvania, and a fifth had been born in Ohio and the other western states. Of the 45% who were foreign-born men, over half came from the German states, and most of the rest came from Great Britain.[18]

Cincinnatians were very conscious of the eclectic composition of the community and gradually developed during the 1830s three general categories to distinguish their fellow-citizens. These categories were defined in terms of nativity, but they also reflected differences in the relative priority and degree of assimilation of each of these three groups. The largest but least distinctive group was the "Buckeyes," predominantly men born in the middle and southern states who had come to Cincinnati early in their careers and had adopted the habits and attitudes of the native-born Ohioans. The smallest but most distinguished group was the "Yankees," the men who came from New England and quickly demonstrated a high degree of social superiority. The third group was the Germans, most of whom came to Cincinnati in the late 1830s and were handicapped by having a foreign language and culture; as a relatively new and alien group, the Germans were considered to be, as yet, inferior to the rest of the inhabitants. In 1840 the Germans were outside the center of the community and somewhat isolated from the English-speaking majority.

Descriptions of the Yankees and Buckeyes found in several recollec-

Table 2.2   Nativity of Cincinnati Male Population, 1840 (%)

	Cist 1841 (N = 12,292)	Shaffer Directory (N = 10,140)	Shaffer Sample (N = 868)
Native Born			
New England	8.1	8.7	9.9
New York-New Jersey	11.9	13.0	13.4
Pennsylvania	9.8	10.8	10.9
Border States	8.0	8.8	7.7
Southern States	5.1	6.0	4.5
Ohio-West	9.7	9.5	12.6
Total	53.0	56.8	59.0
Foreign Born			
England-Scotland	10.0	8.8	9.2
Ireland	6.0	7.1	7.5
Germany	28.0	17.4	18.9
Other European	1.2	2.5	2.9
Total	43.2	35.8	38.5
None Listed	3.8	7.4	2.5
Total	100.0	100.0	100.0
Major Nativity Groups			
Yankees	8.1	8.7	9.9
Buckeyes	44.9	48.1	49.1
Great Britain	16.0	15.9	16.7
Germany	28.0	17.4	18.9

tions of this period unfortunately have a clear Yankee bias, but they suggest that the differences were manifest largely in place of residence in the city and styles of entertainment and that they did not depend strictly on nativity. The Yankees were "a more or less intellectual and artistic set who lived along Fourth Street"; the Buckeyes were "a more or less uncultured and fashionable set who lived on Broadway and east of it." In the latter group there was "a good deal of hard drinking among otherwise decent people," and a special interest in horse racing, sumptuous dinners, and ostentatious display. In the former group, entertainment was "vastly simpler and cleverer and pleasanter. . . . In this circle there was more extemporized dancing and lighter suppers; the clothes were simpler and the talk merrier."[19]

Table 2.3   Priority of Major Nativity Groups
(among Householders Listed in 1840 Directory)

	Yankee (N = 86)	Buckeye (N = 426)	Great Britain (N = 145)	Germany (N = 164)	Total (N = 868)
New settler	55.8	54.9	55.9	76.8	56.3
Old settler	18.6	21.8	20.7	1.8	16.4

The Yankees set the cultural and intellectual tone in the city and, according to some observers at least, seemed to dominate local society. Society here was "more like Boston than any other city in the United States," wrote one eastern visitor to the Queen City: "Conversation was chiefly of a literary cast—free, easy, entertaining, instructive without restraint and without formality." The focus of this Yankee society was the Semi-Colon Club, where prominent professional men like Timothy Walker, James H. Perkins, Salmon P. Chase, and Edward P. Mansfield joined leading local merchants like Nathan Guilford, John P. Foote, and Charles Stetson for literary discussions and light dinners. Although the men born in New England represented only a tenth of the total Cincinnati population in 1840, and had not been in the city as long as the Buckeyes, they were widely reputed to hold an advantageous, influential position. "The great passport to society and its emoluments," wrote a prominent lawyer some years later, "was to *be from New England or of New England birth.*"[20]

According to local legend, Buckeyes were the men who founded most of the financial and commercial operations in the city, and they dominated local society during its early years. This group included Nicholas Longworth and Jacob Burnet from New Jersey, Rev. Joshua Wilson and Charles Hammond from Virginia, and Samuel B. Findlay and James McCandless from Pennsylvania. The focus of Buckeye society was the Buckeye Club, an informal social group organized by Daniel Drake that was composed of the older and more successful men in the community, most of whom came from the middle and southern states. Although by 1840 the Buckeyes may have felt threatened by the intellectual and cultural initiative of the Yankees, the Buckeyes represented a much larger, if somewhat less distinctive, population. Although some observers may have questioned the quality of their society, it is clear that, at least in quantity, the Buckeyes were the predominant group on the Cincinnati scene.[21]

Despite its geographical proximity to the South—the Ohio River later divided the states during the Civil War—Cincinnati was relatively free from any divisive southern influence in its internal affairs. Of the adult male population in 1840, only 5% came from southern states—largely from Virginia—and 9% came from the border states of Maryland, Delaware, and Kentucky. A continuing southern influence could be seen in the split between the New School and Old School Presbyterians during the 1830s more than in any clear sectional division over politics or race relations. Although residents from all sections of the United States, particularly those who traded with the South, agitated for the removal of African Americans in 1829 and against the Abolitionist press of James G. Birney in 1836, it was raiders from across the Ohio River more than local residents with southern sympathies who threatened the free African Americans living in the community. Later, when Cincinnati's prosperity became more dependent on trade with the lower Mississippi Valley, southern sympathies increased, but in 1840 they were hardly evident in the community.[22]

What was unique about the Cincinnati population in 1840 was the large proportion of foreign-born residents, particularly the newly arrived Germans. Since the founding of the city there had been a proportion of emigrants from Europe in the local population, many of whom made important contributions and became prominent members of the community. But before 1830 most of these foreign-born residents were English-speaking emigrants: of the 539 foreign-born inhabitants of Cincinnati in 1825, half came from England, Scotland, and Wales, a third from Ireland, and a tenth from Germany.

This German contingent, although small, included a number of outstanding pioneers: David Ziegler, the first mayor of the town in 1802; Martin Baum, the founder of the Miami Export Bank; and Albert Stein, the builder of the Cincinnati Waterworks. Politically conservative, economically frugal, and relatively well-off, these "Zwanzigers," men who arrived in the 1820s, were careful to soften their native customs and attachments so as not to offend their native-born neighbors. The result was that they fit easily into the total community, were respected and accepted as friends and citizens, and gave Cincinnatians little reason for concern over the arrival of more and more Germans during the late 1830s.[23]

By 1840, however, the proportion of Germans in the total population of Cincinnati had increased tenfold: from 3% in 1825 to 28% in 1840. This was mostly the result of the large influx of Germans in the late 1830s. Cist found more than 14,000 Germans living in the city, including 3,440 men. This increase in the size and proportion of the German group in the total population was largely the result of difficulties in the German states during the 1830s and the favorable reports about Cincinnati that the Zwanzigers sent to their friends and relatives.

Consequently, during the 1830s, particularly during the last five years of the decade, over 10,000 German immigrants, *Dreissigern,* arrived in the Queen City. Cincinnatians welcomed these new arrivals but soon found them very different from the Zwanzigers they had come to know and accept. Not surprisingly, the newly arrived Germans generally did not speak English and tended to live and associate with their own kind, whom they could understand and whose habits were similar to their own. This natural tendency of the Dreissigern to cluster together resulted in a lack of communication between the new immigrants and the natives that created a division between the German-speaking and English-speaking members of the community.

Before 1840, this separation of the German immigrants from the rest of the Cincinnati community, and the resulting sense of alienation and antagonism, was not considered to be serious or permanent. Cincinnatians welcomed the assistance of the Dreissigern in the work of building the city, readily accepted their money in payment for household goods, food, and rent, and appreciated their contribution to the city's rapid progress and prosperity. Compared to the Zwanzigers, the Dreissigern, who had a strong admiration and affection for President Andrew Jackson, seemed radical politically, but the majority had not yet registered to vote or consolidated their political strength to a degree that was evident in elections before 1840. Although the Dreissigern had organized certain German activities such as a singing group and a militia company, started their own newspapers, and were largely responsible for the growing numbers of Catholics in the community, these distinctly German influences were not yet clearly visible to the larger English-speaking community. As long as these new German immigrants worked hard, were law-abiding, and did not threaten the dominant position of the native-born citizens, their peculiar customs and alleged clannishness were tolerated by the majority of Cincinnatians.[24]

Population Composition: Heads of Families and Boarders

"Cheerful, thriving, and animated" were the words Charles Dickens used to describe Cincinnati after his visit in 1842. The dynamic atmosphere in the city was the result of its distinctive demographic composition. As one contemporary observer wrote some years later: "The population, being composed of recent immigrants, was made up to be a great extent of persons of youth or early manhood. . . . Such an amount of youthful blood gave a peculiar air of life and activity to the city."[25]

This distinctive vitality was largely the result of the large number of young adults, particularly men, living in the city in 1840. Almost half of the total white population of 43,096 fell within the twenty to fifty age range, and males represented 60.1% of this group. Of the 13,705 adult white males, over half, 7,321, were in their twenties; another third, 3,800, were in their thirties; and over a tenth, 1,496, were in their forties: together, these 12,617 men between the ages of twenty and fifty represented 29.3% of the total white population of the city. This concentration of men was half again as great as the population of men between twenty and fifty in the national white population, 19.2%, and was greater than that of most major cities in the United States in 1840.[26]

The Cincinnati population of 1840 was also marked by a relatively low proportion of children. Just over a third of the total white population was under fifteen years of age, and the number of children under five years, 6,807, was considerably greater than those between five and ten years, 4,171, or those between ten and fifteen years, 3,828. This narrow demographic base of the Cincinnati population was largely the result of the city's rapid growth, the youthfulness of the adult population, and the fact that, as Cist noted, young couples generally put off starting a family until after they had been settled for several years.[27]

Cincinnati also had a remarkably small proportion of older residents in the 1840 population. The number of residents in their fifties (1,402), sixties (679), and seventies (218), and those older than seventy (43) together represented less than 5% of the total white population at this time. Visitors often commented on the absence of old people and beggars

Table 2.4 Cincinnati Population Composition, 1840

	Under 5	5–10	10–15	15–20	20–30	30–40	40–50	50–60	60–70	70–80	80 and over	Total
Total white population (N)	6,807	4,171	3,828	4,924	12,558	5,517	2,949	1,402	679	218	43	43,096
% of total population	15.8	9.7	8.9	11.4	29.1	12.8	6.8	3.2	1.6	.5	.09	100.0%
Men (N)	—	—	—	—	7,321	3,800	1,495	673	302	92	21	13,705
% male	50.7	49.5	47.4	45.0	58.3	68.9	50.7	48.0	44.5	42.2	38.8	52.7
Relationship of local to national % of population (same = 100.00)	90.6	68.4	73.5	105.6	160.2	110.8	93.3	74.7	64.3	34.4	—	100.0

Sources: For Cincinnati data: *Compendium of the . . . Sixth Census* (Washington, 1841), 76–77; for national population: *Statistical View . . . A Compendium of the Seventh Census* (Washington, 1854), 51–57.

on the streets of the Queen City; it was, as Cist remarked, "a rare thing to see an old man" in this booming western city.[28]

Cincinnati's white population of 43,096 was distributed among 8,265 census families. In 89.1% of these families the family head was a man; the average age of these male heads of families was approximately thirty-five. Over three-quarters of these census families, 6,908, had between two and seven members, only 172 families were composed of a single individual, and only 216 families had more than twelve members. The average size of these 8,265 census families was between four and five members (the mean was 5.11; the median was 4.27).[29]

The large majority of the 8,049 families with less than thirteen members appear to have been families in the conventional sense, composed of a pair of adults of comparable ages, children, and, in some cases, additional adults. Over half of these families, 4,259, had a single male and female adult; 3,350 of these families also had children. In 1,130 of these 8,049 families there was either no man or no woman present: since 986 of these incomplete families included children they were probably conventional families with one parent absent or dead. Finally, 2,658 of these 8,049 families included at least three adult members: 1,416 of these families had a single extra adult, generally a woman; 269 of them had a single extra adult, generally a man; 269 of these families had a pair of adults of each sex and corresponding ages, who were probably two married couples; and the remaining 973 families had at least two additional members who were not a married couple.[30]

The 216 census families with more than twelve members were not conventional families but seem rather to have been large boardinghouses, hotels, and public institutions. Most of the city's large transient dwellings were located near the river, where over half of the large census families were enumerated, and served the many visitors, rivermen, and other itinerants who filled this area. There were also a number of other large boardinghouses scattered throughout the city that served as an initial, temporary home for newcomers who had just arrived in Cincinnati. Although these 216 large census families represented less than 3% of the total census families in 1840, they included over 12% of the total population and over a quarter of the 13,705 men.[31]

The 7,364 male heads of census families, therefore, represent only slightly more than half of the total 13,705 adult white males enumerated in the 1840 census. The remaining 6,341 men were living as relatives, friends, employees, or boarders in census families they did not head. Over half of these boarders, 3,522 men, lived in the large transient quarters. The heads of families, representing 53.4% of the total adult white male population, and the boarders, representing 46.6%, differed in several important demographic and psychological respects that suggest a basic division within the Cincinnati adult white male population in 1840.[32]

Demographically, the 7,364 heads of families were generally older, married, and living in their own single-family households, while the 6,341 boarders were characteristically younger, single, and living in large boardinghouses or hotels. More than 70% of the family heads were over thirty years of age but more than 80% of the boarders were in their twenties. Nearly every family head lived in a household with a female adult of comparable age, who was probably his wife. Most of the boarders seem to have been single: in the large census families with more than twelve members, where 3,522 of the boarders lived, the ratio of men to women was nearly 6 to 1; in the census families with fewer than thirteen members, where the rest of the boarders lived, there were generally not additional females of comparable age present. These were the "numbers of young and unmarried men" Cist pointed to when he reviewed the composition of the city's population, and their presence gave Cincinnati its distinctively dynamic character.[33]

Cist also pointed to an important psychological difference between the heads of families and the boarders when he remarked that the latter group were "testing the advantages of the measure [of settling in Cincinnati] at the least expense." The severe housing shortage in Cincinnati at this time made it difficult and expensive to rent or buy a home, and newcomers seem to have put off this decision until they were committed to settling in the city. Boardinghouses and hotels provided cheap temporary quarters for the newcomers during the months, and even years, that were required to find a satisfactory job, make friends, and decide to settle permanently in the city. Homes, on the other hand, represented a greater commitment of time and money and were acquired only after several years of residence in Cincinnati. The boarders differed from the heads of families psychologically, therefore, in that they generally lacked the family responsibilities and sense of commitment that characterized the householders.[34]

The Boarders: A Closer Examination

The fact that Cist found 13,705 adult white males during his census enumeration in the summer of 1840 while Shaffer, the preceding summer, included only 8,684 men in his *Directory* raises the question of why these two figures for the Cincinnati population around 1840 differed so greatly. The difference of more than 5,000 men cannot simply be explained by the rapid growth of the city during this one-year period; rather, it suggests that these two sources represent the Cincinnati population according to somewhat different criteria. A comparison of the demographic composition of the census and the *Directory for 1840* reveals not only that the former was much larger in size than the latter but also, and more important, that Cist included certain groups that Shaffer generally excluded.

The number of men listed in the 1840 *Directory*, 8,684, represents only 63.4% of the total number of adult white males, 13,705, Cist enumerated in the 1840 census. Of the 8,684 men included in the directory, 7,027 were heads of families and 1,657 were boarders. The 7,027 directory male heads of families represent 95.5% of the 7,364 male heads of families listed in the census: the fact that Shaffer and Cist found a comparable number of heads of families suggests that these figures are fairly accurate and that the difference of 337 male heads of families is a good measure of the actual increase in the number of families during this one-year period. The 1,657 directory boarders, however, represent only 26.2% of the 6,341 boarders enumerated in the census: this discrepancy suggests that Shaffer underrepresented, Cist overrepresented, or both misrepresented the actual number of boarders in Cincinnati in 1840.[35]

The considerable difference between the size of the population enumerated in the *Directory for 1840* and in *Cincinnati in 1841* therefore, occurred largely because Cist included a much larger proportion of boarders than Shaffer: the 6,341 census boarders represent 46.6% of the 13,705 adult white males Cist found, while the 1,657 directory boarders represent only 19.4% of the 8,684 men included by Shaffer. It is unlikely that the proportion of boarders in Cincinnati increased by this extent between 1839 and 1840, or that all 5,000 excluded boarders actually arrived in the city after Shaffer made his survey but before Cist took the census. Rather, this suggests that boarders were included in the census but excluded from the *Directory* because the purpose of these two sources differed.

According to the federal census instructions, Cist was to enumerate every person who considered Cincinnati to be his home, but it was not necessary that he be an active or permanent resident of the community. According to the title page of the *Directory,* Shaffer listed the "house-holders, heads of families, and those engaged in business," clearly a more exclusive and established portion of the total population. Cist was paid according to the number of inhabitants he enumerated: this financial advantage, combined with his strong booster spirit, no doubt prompted him to include as many people as possible in the census. Shaffer, however, was publishing a directory that he hoped to sell to local businessmen; this, combined with his lack of experience in doing this kind of work, probably led him to concentrate on the more prominent and permanent members of the community.

Therefore, boarders were probably excluded from the *Directory* because Shaffer did not consider them to be settled, established members of the community, but they were included in the census because Cist wanted to enumerate as large a population as possible. As single young men living in transient dwellings, the boarders were of little particular interest to the local businessmen; as a group of approximately 5,000 workers and consumers, however, they added considerably to the growth and prosperity of the city. The question remains who these boarders were and what their status in Cincinnati was in 1840. A comparison of the nativity and occupational composition of the census and *Directory* helps to answer these questions and suggests that the boarders stood in a marginal position in relation to the more settled, established house-holders of the community.

There is one major nativity group, the Germans, and one major occupational group, the rivermen, represented in very different proportions in the census and *Directory.* The 1,764 Germans included in the directory represent only 52.8% of the 3,340 Germans Cist found in 1840: this suggests that Shaffer did not include approximately 1,500 Germans, probably because they had not yet arrived or settled when he made his directory survey. The 304 rivermen listed in the directory represent only 17.4% of the 1,748 "men engaged in navigation" reported in the 1840 census: this suggests that Shaffer excluded a comparable number of rivermen, probably because they were in the city only

Table 2.5   Comparison of Census and *Directory* Population, 1840

	Census	Directory for 1840	Directory Census (%)
Total heads of families	8,265	7,494	90.7
Male heads of families	7,364	7,027	95.5
Male boarders	6,341	1,654	26.2
Total males	13,705	8,681	63.4
Germans	3,340	1,764	52.8
Rivermen	1,764	304	17.4

periodically and did not have permanent homes. Approximately 30% of these boarders, therefore, were German newcomers who hoped to settle in Cincinnati; another 30% of these boarders were transient rivermen who were not really residents of the city at this time.

Since there were few Germans who were rivermen, these two groups make up the majority of the approximately 5,000 boarders enumerated by Cist but not listed by Shaffer. The remaining excluded boarders, approximately 2,000 men, are impossible to identify, but they were probably either native-born newcomers who hoped to settle in Cincinnati or itinerant workers who were in the city when Cist took the census. Thus, in 1840 there were roughly 1,000 young men who had just arrived from their homes in the East or the rural areas surrounding the city. Similarly, there were roughly 1,000 men who were in Cincinnati temporarily during the summer of 1840, either on business or paying visits, whom Cist included in his census enumeration in order to inflate the total population.

The analysis indicates that the difference between the *Directory* and census populations of approximately 5,000 men was due largely to Cist's decision to include, while Shaffer had excluded, a large number of boarders. Roughly half of these boarders were newcomers, predominantly German immigrants, who had not arrived or settled when Shaffer made his survey but hoped to become permanent residents of the city. The remaining half of the boarders were transients, particularly rivermen, who were omitted by Shaffer because they had no established place of work or residence in the city and could not be considered part of the settled community in 1840. Each group was excluded from the *Directory* but included in the census for a different reason, therefore, and each represented a distinctive group with a marginal position in Cincinnati in 1840.

It is possible now to return to the general discussion of the rapid growth of the Cincinnati population during the late 1830s and, particularly, the size, character, and status of the large group of newcomers. This analysis suggests that there were approximately 5,000 newcomers who were predominantly boarders, single young men who had not yet settled, or transient workers, when Shaffer made his directory survey. These newcomers were excluded from the 1840 *Directory* because they had no established place of residence or business. The distinguishing characteristic of the newcomers, however, was more their transient or unsettled status than their recent arrival in the city, although these two factors were closely related. The total number of boarders in 1840 was actually greater, and the number of men who arrived within a year of the census was probably smaller, than 5,000, but this is an estimate of the number of men who were not part of the settled, established community in 1840.

A Magnetic Field Model of the Cincinnati Population

Although *priority* is an arbitrary measure of the relative length of adult residence in the city—based on the indirect and imprecise criterion of inclusion in the 1840 directory and those preceding it—it suggests relative differences within the population according to a variety of related demographic and psychological characteristics. Comparing the newcomers, the new settlers, and the old settlers reflects not only differences in the relative length of adult residence in the city but also, and more important, relative differences in age, family status, type of residence, nativity, and identity and commitment as a Cincinnatian. Although these distinctions may represent only vague disparities in degree on an individual level, they suggest two important differences in kind on an aggregate level that divide the Cincinnati population in 1840.

The dissimilarities between the newcomers, new settlers, and old settlers suggest two basic divisions within the Cincinnati adult white male population in 1840. First, within the total population of 13,705 men enumerated in the 1840 census, there was a division between the majority of householders, most of whom were included in the 1840

Directory, and the minority of newcomers, who were generally excluded from the directory. This reflects significant differences in age, family status, and type of residence and also suggests important differences in nativity, length of residence in the city, and sense of identity and commitment as a Cincinnatian. Second, within the more settled, established community, there was a division between the majority of householders who had arrived in Cincinnati sometime after 1830, most of whom were new settlers, and the minority of old settlers who had been adult residents of the community for at least a decade. This division also represents differences in age, experience, and degree of identity and commitment as a Cincinnatian.

It is possible to describe the total number of 13,705 adult white male Cincinnatians as existing within a large circular magnetic field in which their relative priority as newcomers, new settlers, and old settlers defines their respective positions. The approximately 1,500 old settlers form the core of the circle because of their greater age, experience, and sense of identity and commitment as Cincinnatians. The approximately 5,000 newcomers would form an outer ring, outside of the established community of householders, because of their unsettled, uncommitted status as single young men without homes of their own. Finally, the remaining 7,000 householders, including the 5,000 new settlers, would form a middle ring—within the community because of their settled, established status but outside the core of the old settlers because of their relative lack of experience and identity or commitment as Cincinnatians.

This magnetic field model describes some of the important demographic and psychological differences within the adult white male population of Cincinnati in 1840. This model is a horizontal magnetic field because it is designed to suggest relative forces within an essentially open, fluid environment. It is intended to illustrate how certain basic demographic differences represented in priority—age, family status, type of residence—are related to the way and degree to which the central values, or community ideology, attract the individuals within the magnetic field, and how these individuals relate to one another, or the particular spheres and sectors of social interaction.

As mentioned, the old settlers, who stand out within the general community of householders because of their relatively greater age and experience, form the core of the magnetic field. Over the years these men had developed a sense of group cohesion, based on familiarity and shared

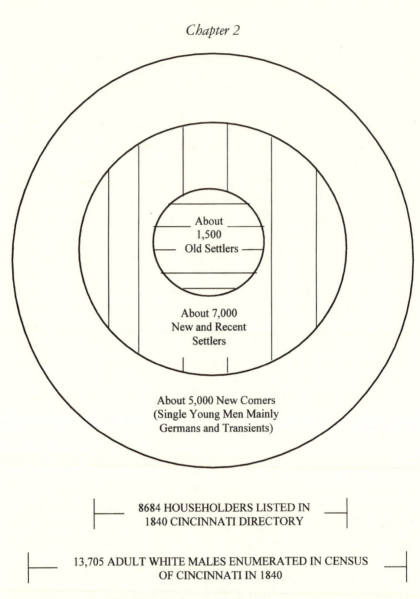

About
1,500
Old Settlers

About 7,000
New and Recent
Settlers

About 5,000 New Comers
(Single Young Men Mainly
Germans and Transients)

8684 HOUSEHOLDERS LISTED IN
1840 CINCINNATI DIRECTORY

13,705 ADULT WHITE MALES ENUMERATED IN CENSUS
OF CINCINNATI IN 1840

Magnetic Field Model of Cincinnati Adult White Population in 1840

experiences, that gave them a common identity; during this period they
also formed a strong attachment to the city, based on direct involvement
in its growth and prosperity, that resulted in a strong degree of commitment. These were the men who articulated the community ideology,
drawn from their own personal experiences, and they were probably the

ones who identified with it most strongly. As will be described, these were the men who formed a good portion of the successful, wealthy merchants and professionals who, probably because of their greater age and experience, played a major role in the associational life of the community. Old settlers like Jacob Burnet, Charles Cist, Daniel Drake, and Nathan Guilford clearly stood at the center of the local society, forming its heart.

The newcomers, conversely, were a marginal group because of their relative youth and lack of established roots or associations within the community. Their situation around the periphery of the magnetic field, outside the more stable, established community of householders, reflects both their distinctive demographic character as young, single, unsettled men and their concomitant psychological orientation as new, often alien or transient, and uncommitted residents. Their position on the periphery of the community suggests, further, that they had relatively little contact or communication with the householders and felt the least sense of identity as Cincinnatians. Because the newcomers generally did not interact with the householders and did not identify strongly with the prevailing community ideology, they tended to exist, in many respects, as isolated, anonymous outsiders.

The majority of the newcomers were either German immigrants or transient workers. These outsiders were probably the most alienated, socially and ideologically, from the general community, but because they were identified either as foreigners or transients, they seem to have had strong independent group identities that made assimilation particularly difficult for these two groups. In an earlier period, when the city was smaller and more homogeneous in composition, newcomers like Timothy Walker, Flamen Ball, and even Charles Reemlin had wanted both to remain with fellow newcomers and to become a part of the dominant community. By 1840, however, the newcomers seemed to be more alienated and the community more antagonistic, and the Germans and the transients tended to coalesce into separate and increasingly incompatible groups of their own rather than assimilating.

Contemporary accounts suggest that both the Germans and transients formed fairly clearly defined groups in Cincinnati which were, according to these observers, largely independent of the dominant English-speaking community. The Germans tended to congregate in certain areas and form their own social groups. Despite the efforts of assimilators like

Calvin Stowe, they did not usually send their children to the public schools, and they attended their own Catholic churches. When they did vote, they seem to have opposed the prevailing confident, corporate concept of local government. This marginal, independent position and the concomitant sense of alienation it produced is dramatically illustrated by Cist in a story about a German who was left out of the city directory:

> I had been preparing for publication, a directory, and in the process of the work, called upon an honest German up Walnut Street, who was extensively engaged in the manufacture of bratwurst, knackwurst, leber wurst, and sourkrout. I had taken down his address. "When you got dat book out," said he, "you brings me one, and I pays for it." I promised to do so accordingly. By some unaccountable neglect of my transcriber of names, the dealer in wurst and sour-krout was left out of the directory, and having ascertained that fact, I did not trouble myself to deliver a book, which I knew this individual would not take on finding himself left out, as he readily would by turning to it in search of the name—the universal practice of purchasers. Several months had elapsed, when one morning rising Main Street, and just opposite Ephraim Morgan's store, I discovered my German friend. Stopping short, and in a very angry tone, he accosted me with, "Why you not put my name down in your correctory?" "Well, I don't know; is it not down?" was my remark. "No," replied he, very indignantly, "Your correctory not wort one cent. How do people knows where he kits his sour-krout?"

This omission, multiplied hundreds of times, reflected and reinforced the general lack of communication and sense of isolation of the Germans.[36]

The transients were also described by local observers as having formed a clearly defined and separate group in Cincinnati at this time. In 1839 Alonzo Garcelon, a young medical student from Maine, spent a year in the Queen City and recorded his impressions of the local society. In a long letter he provided a vivid description of the transient population as an infestation of the riverfront area: "Here you will find a floating population with the curse of Jehovah upon them, a migratory character, and without position, names, or homes. In the spring you will see them in flocks, like our wild geese of the North, leaving the South and locating themselves in the cities and towns along the Ohio and upper Mississippi, getting their living by gambling, robbery, thieving, and polluting *what otherwise might* be a virtuous and respectable community." Garcelon's description of this "floating population" and their nefarious activities is substantiated by the numerous newspaper accounts of low life in the riverfront area. This vision of the riverfront also appears in James H. Perkins's stories describing the dangerous lures of liquor, gambling, and vice that enticed young men when they first arrived in the city. It is evident that the transients formed another large group in the Cincinnati population that was considered a threat to the "virtuous and respectable community."[37]

The approximately 7,000 householders who had been adult residents of Cincinnati for less than a decade in 1840 formed the third major group in the local population and can be described as forming the middle ring of the magnetic field. As settled, established heads of families, who generally had their own homes and regular jobs, these householders were distinct from the newly arrived or transient newcomers, but because they lacked the age and experience of the old settlers, they probably did not have the same degree of identity and commitment as Cincinnatians. The intermediate status of these stable householders is based primarily on the fact that they lived in their own homes; as Cist put it: "in these walls dwell the middle class—everywhere the bone and sinew of society."[38]

These 7,000 householders represent over half of the total adult white male population in 1840 and over 80% of the settled, established community. The question remains whether they felt any common sense of identity or group interest and can thus be defined as a distinct class; or whether they existed as a generally unorganized, unclass-conscious mass of individuals held together only by being socially repelled by the newcomers and rejected by the old settlers. Inclusion in the city directory gave them a sense of identity, but only with time could they establish the various ties necessary for a real sense of group consciousness. Since approximately 5,000 of these 7,000 householders were new settlers who had been in the community for only a few years, the majority had probably not had the time to develop these ties by 1840.

The magnetic field model identifies, on the basis of priority and related demographic characteristics, four fairly distinctive and independent groups within the Cincinnati population in 1840: the old settlers, the new settlers, the German newcomers, and the transients. Further, it indicates how the particular demographic composition of these four groups was manifest in certain distinctive ideological attitudes and patterns of social behavior. The purpose of this analysis is to demonstrate that these demographic differences define the fundamental divisions

within the local population and that the differences between the newcomers and householders and the relative priority of the householders
represented the most important lines defining the Cincinnati social
structure in 1840. Although the four groups are somewhat arbitrary and
artificial, Cincinnatians recognized such distinctions, and they were influential in the ongoing life of the community.

Strains within the Social Order

Rapid population growth and diversification are basic in the development of boomtowns and central to the understanding of the Jacksonian
America. The remarkable vitality, volatility, and variety of the Cincinnati population in 1840 is, in fact, one of the distinguishing characteristics of nineteenth-century urbanization and westward expansion.
Because Cincinnati was the fastest growing American city during this
period, and because it was the first major German urban center, it may be
that these three demographic characteristics first coincided in a concentrated context in Cincinnati. Whether the first and most dynamic cosmopolitan city in the nineteenth century was Cincinnati, or whether
instead it was Philadelphia, New York, Boston, or New Orleans, it is
clear that these particular demographic forces created major strains in
the social order in Cincinnati during the 1840s, strains that became
common in American cities by midcentury.[39]

During the 1830s Cincinnatians gradually became aware of the social
consequences of their city's rapid development. While local leaders welcomed the newcomers, who, they argued, would quickly assimilate
themselves into the existing order, they also came to recognize that the
large influx of immigrants created, at least temporarily, a sense of disloca-
tion and disorientation. As the editor of the *Cincinnati Journal,* Rev.
Thomas Brainard, noted in 1834: "So rapidly has our city enlarged itself
and such is the migratory character of our citizens that we are almost
strangers to one another." As the annual rate of population growth multiplied from approximately one thousand during the first half of the
decade to nearly four thousand by 1840, not knowing one's fellow residents became a more and more pervasive situation.[40]

The arrival of a large number of German immigrants in the late 1830s
compounded the problem. Despite Francis Trollope's bitter comments
about her reception in the Queen City in 1828, most foreign observers

commended Cincinnatians during the 1830s for their friendly, open, and hospitable attitude toward visitors. Their descriptions of the cold, impersonal manner in which Cincinnatians treated one another suggest a very different pattern of social relations. As an observer remarked in 1834, "Accustomed constantly to see emigrants, with whom they form new acquaintances, they show a degree of indifference to each other, and this characteristic influences their actions, and stamps them with a certain want of feeling." By 1840, when James S. Buckingham visited Cincinnati, the situation was apparently worse, and his only criticism of the community was the prevailing atmosphere of incompatibility:

> They seemed to me, with very few exceptions, the coldest, most apathetic, and least hospitable of all the people we have met with in the Union; and I do not think there is any city in the country, the inhabitants of which think so highly of themselves, and affect such superiority over strangers and foreigners, as Cincinnati; though they are nearly all of them strangers themselves, being a collection of persons from all parts of the globe, from every section of the Union, and more heterogeneous perhaps than any other 50,000 persons settled on any other spot.

Buckingham was not complaining about his own reception or that of other distinguished guests, which was always very cordial; rather, he was describing the way in which most Cincinnatians had become hardened to one another as a result of the pressures of dynamic and diversified population growth.[41]

Increasing concern over crime and a growing demand for "law and order" in the community were the first manifestations of this tension. Complaints about criminal activity and calls for greater police protection appear throughout the history of Cincinnati, but there was a marked rise in the level of concern over these problems around 1840. According to Garcelon, Cincinnatians generally denied or belittled such problems, at least to visitors, in fear that they would dissuade newcomers from settling in the city. But in 1840 Mayor Samuel W. Davies was forced to admit in his annual report to city council that Cincinnati had become "a favorite rendezvous" of "bad persons" and that his police force could not handle the problem.[42]

The main source of the problem, according to the Cincinnati *Gazette,* was the "large floating population of pilferers and vagrants" who congregated in the city. These transients were charged with most of the robberies, assaults, gambling, and other vices that offended the respectable members of the community. As an "Old Resident" wrote, it was such "objectionable" types who were largely responsible for the firecrackers, cigar smoking, and sleds on the streets, and immoral activity on the Sabbath. These conditions continued, and Cincinnatians continued to complain; the effect was an increasing recognition of the undesirable qualities of certain portions of the local population.[43]

By the early 1840s it was evident which groups were considered responsible for the increasing problems in Cincinnati. Pauperism, a major source of crime and corruption, was confined largely to two groups: the Germans and the transients. In 1841, of the 1,034 paupers reported in the city, 560 were foreigners while only 474 were native-born, and 744 were nonresidents while only 290 were residents. By 1842 the number of paupers had increased to 1,261, with three-quarters of them foreigners and nonresidents. It is not surprising that, merited or not, Cincinnatians became increasingly antagonistic and open in their attacks on these two particular groups.[44]

In a general review of the deteriorating situation by 1845, the editor of the Cincinnati *Commercial* commented that three-quarters of the Cincinnati population were very moral and law-abiding; "the other fourth are not." Not all of the troublemakers, however, were Germans and transients. The Fly Market Rangers—a notorious gang with reputed Whig affiliations that operated in the riverfront area—included, according to the Cincinnati *Enquirer,* a local drayman, constable, and Third Street broker, although its leader, Alfred Allen, and his brother were rivermen who lived in their mother's boardinghouse. The Fly Market Rangers focused its energies on the Germans—who, as foreigners, Catholics, and Democrats, were triply damned—and probably had some support from the nativists in the community.[45]

In the early 1840s a series of riots in Cincinnati brought to the surface the growing group antagonism and general tension. Riots before this period, particularly the Anti-Negro Riot of 1829 and the Anti-Abolitionist Riot of 1836 (the Birney Riot), had been attacks by the community, sanctioned by local leaders, on groups or individuals considered a threat to the prevailing social order. The riots that occurred during the 1840s, however, were attacks by one peripheral group against another, and community leaders generally condemned such groups for disturbing the prevailing social order. These riots reflect, therefore, the crystallization of group identity on the part of the peripheral population of the city and a growing fear of "mobocracy" on the part of the stable, established members of the community.

In September 1841—after more than a decade of relative racial peace in the city, during which time the African American community developed a strong internal structure and sense of group identity—a group of Irishmen tangled with some African Americans on the corner of Sixth Street and Broadway. Sporadic fights between these two groups, who lived in close proximity in the First and Third Wards along the eastern edge of the city, broke out in the area. These isolated encounters developed into a general riot, however, when a large mob, said to be led by rivermen and Kentuckians who were not residents of the community, formed and rampaged through the African American section of Cincinnati, destroying several homes and shops. The respectable members of the community rallied immediately against both groups; and the mayor, police, and local militia companies finally managed to contain them and establish control. Both groups were equally denounced in the press and by city council for their actions and for disrupting the community.[46]

The following year, in August 1842, came the first "German Riot." The initial cause of the riot is unclear, but seems to have been the way in which members of the Jagers, a German volunteer militia company, reacted when some boys harassed them on their way home from a drill. A crowd of angry men gathered at the Sans Souci Hotel, owned by the company commander, and began to hurl bricks into the building. The German soldiers inside responded with gunfire, and several men in the crowd, including a constable, were wounded. The mayor arrived, finally secured order, and then arrested thirteen of the German soldiers. The German community gathered in a large public meeting to protest that they were the victims of an attack by "the ignorant and brutal part of the native-born community." Although the German soldiers were soon exonerated in court, the affair had a lasting impact on the German population of Cincinnati, which became more separatist and militant than before. At the same time, it increased the level of hostility toward Germans, and cries of "The Dutch will take the city!" were now openly expressed.[47]

The same year Cincinnati experienced the Bank Riot, which resulted from the suspension of several local banks. This riot involved members of the established community, since they were the victims of the failure, and they seem to have been responsible for the damage caused when the buildings were sacked. The mayor once again called for order, but this time he was less successful. One local militia company refused to take any action and the City Guard, led by Captain Ormsby M. Mitchel, had trouble dispersing the crowd. In the aftermath of the affair local editors decried the violence but generally refused to point to any individuals or groups. Instead, the mayor and city council were blamed for not taking more decisive action. In this case, the press refused to condemn the rioters, who appear to have been solid members of the community who had lost their savings, and criticized local officials for a lack of authority.[48]

These riots revealed the divisions and increasing antagonism in Cincinnati after 1840 and helped to define the particular groups within the general population. Germans and transients were blamed for the increasing level of violence and soon came to be identified by the more stable, established members of the community as threats to the prevailing social order. But, as the Bank Riot demonstrated, respectable householders were also capable of mob actions, although in this case the definition of social order became blurred. This suggests that the widespread and growing outcry against "mobocracy" was more an attack on groups in the community that were considered troublesome than a blanket condemnation of violence. Peter Zinn, a young lawyer, condemned both parties in the Anti-Negro Riot of 1829, declaring "The mob, not the people, is beginning to rule," but failed to blame the mob in the Bank Riot, noting "some good done through a great deal of injury." Violence in support of an understandable grievance, as in the case of the Bank Riot, and particularly in the name of community harmony, as in the Birney Riot, was acceptable; violence between disreputable groups in the city was not.[49]

It was the temperance movement, however, that defined the divisions in the Cincinnati population most clearly and gave the established members of the community their clearest sense of group identity. Local legislation against the licensing of coffeehouses had been the first expression of this movement, but the defeat of the anti-coffeehouse candidates in 1841 did not mark the end of the crusade. Rather, it moved the issue from the political arena to the realm of moral suasion, where temperance reformers seemed to be less concerned with solving the problem than publicly defining who stood where on the question. The main thrust of the "Washingtonians" was to get citizens to sign the "Temperance Pledge": "In joining the Temperance Society I do it only with the hope of procuring others to sign. I am satisfied that I have done my duty, and what is best for myself and those few over whom I might have the least influence." The Washingtonians, according to Peter Zinn, were motivated by their general concern that "Spiritous liquors is [*sic*] a great injury to the community." But their strategy was geared more toward identifying their supporters, who were strongly persuaded to sign their pledge, than toward attacking the drinkers and the drinking houses directly. Consequently, temperance advocates measured their success by the number of citizens, 8,000, who had signed the pledge, not by the number of drinkers reformed or coffeehouses closed, which, in fact, they could not claim.[50]

The riots and the temperance movement of the early 1840s, therefore, illustrate how the Cincinnati population operated within the magnetic field model. The two peripheral groups—the Germans and the transients—were considered to be the main sources of lawlessness, intemperance, and violence in the city, and the more stable, established members of the community mobilized a general campaign to identify and isolate them through their condemnation of "mobocracy" and demands for temperance. The significance of these efforts, however, was not so much to resolve the alleged problems, which continued throughout the mid-nineteenth century, as it was to develop a strong, distinctive sense of common identity within the community composed of householders with diverse backgrounds, many of whom were new settlers.

After 1840, as the inherent tension between population growth and social order became more evident, Cincinnatians came to define their community less in terms of the city's general progress and prosperity and more in terms of certain personal attitudes and forms of behavior. Rather than considering all of the people as part of the community, they came to consider only the more stable, established residents who conformed to the dominant social ideology as the real community. It is significant that during the 1840s there were increasing references to a more exclusive community within the larger population, such as the *Commercial* editorial on the three-quarters of the population who were law-abiding and moral, the Washingtonians' claim that they had the support of three-quarters of the adult population, and Buckingham's contention that two-thirds of the Cincinnati population were affiliated with a church.

The new community of interests within a larger population of residents that emerged during the 1840s was defined according to moral rather than economic or social criteria. This community was described as the "respectable community," the "virtuous people," the "good society," and the "responsible citizens." The moral criteria for inclusion in this community were never explicitly defined, but they clearly depended on a certain degree of ideological and behavioral conformity. As one Cincinnatian put it, in defining the requirements of society during this period, "Certain conventional rules . . . had to be obeyed, which formed a great safeguard." This kind of conformity depended on a certain identity and commitment to the dominant local values (ideology), which depended, in turn, on a certain length of stable residence in the city (priority).[51]

It is significant that this new self-defined community was described in moral rather than social or economic terms. By focusing on the common elements of identity and experience, it was possible to overlook certain differences in background. By emphasizing a common interest in social order it was possible to ignore other distinctions. As the Washingtonians declared: "In this cause, at least, all sects and all parties are united. Let us go heart and hand, together, a united people."[52] By uniting in opposition to the threatening groups within the population, it was possible to forge a loose common bond that transcended, at least temporarily, the growing structural inequalities that existed within the community.

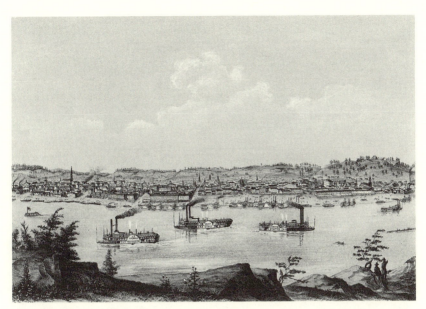

Otto Onken, view of Cincinnati. Courtesy Cincinnati Historical Society.

John Casper Wild, view of Cincinnati from Covington, Kentucky. Courtesy Cincinnati Historical Society.

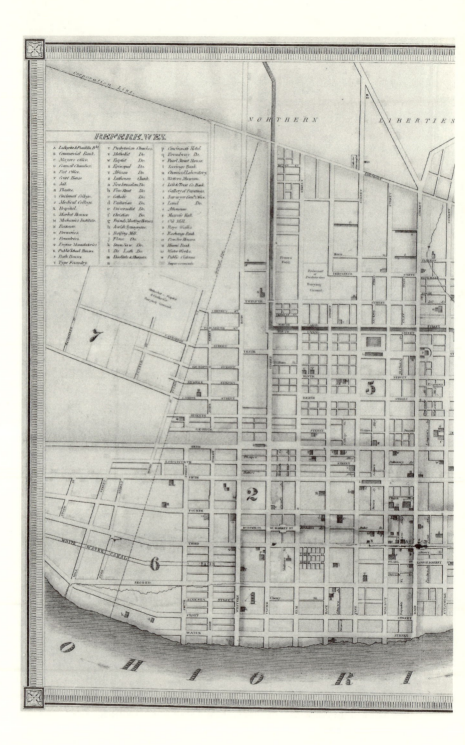

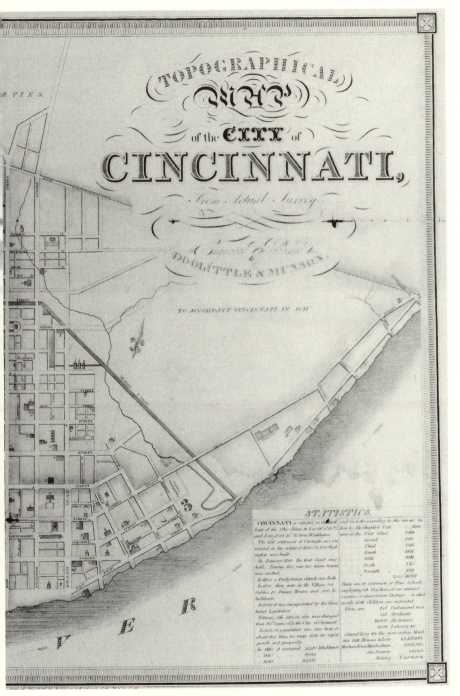

Topographical map of Cincinnati. Author's collection.

Otto Onken, Public Landing. Courtesy Cincinnati Historical Society.

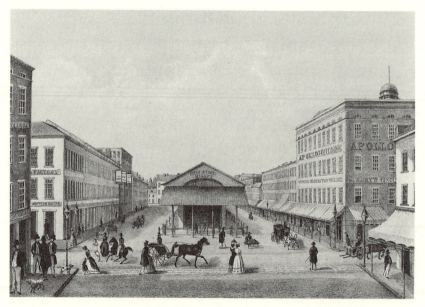

Otto Onken, Fifth Street Market. Courtesy Cincinnati Historical Society.

Otto Onken, Main Street, between Fourth and Fifth. Courtesy Cincinnati Historical Society.

Otto Onken, Broadway. Courtesy Cincinnati Historical Society.

Otto Onken, Burnet House. Courtesy Cincinnati Historical Society.

Otto Onken, Third Street, between Main and Vine. Courtesy Cincinnati Historical Society.

3

✍

The Masses and the Classes: Social Structure

The sound of her workmen, in every street,
Is heard—and contentment we every where meet;
And each one is striving to get all he can;
For money, dear money's the making of man.

Ye merry MECHANICS, come join in my song,
And let the brisk chorus go bounding along;
Tho' some may be poor, and some rich there may be,
Yet all are contented, and happy, and free!

May each *Trade & Profession* join heart and hand;
To cherish the *Arts* and keep *Peace* through the land
Each *Apprentice* and *Journeyman* join in the song,
And let the brisk chorus go bounding along.

—EXCERPTS FROM DAVID SHAFFER,
"RHYMES TO SUIT THE TIMES," 1840

"Life in Cincinnati in 1840"

After eight years of personal experience and observation, James H. Perkins described his new adopted home in a short story entitled "Life in Cincinnati in 1840." Scion of a distinguished old New England family, Perkins had come to Cincinnati in 1832, at the age of twenty-two, to escape the cold, harsh Boston atmosphere and explore the possibilities for success in the West. He spent several years studying law with Timothy Walker, moved on to edit a local literary journal, engaged in an abortive manufacturing enterprise, turned to the scientific practice of horticulture on a small farm he bought just north of the city, served as part-time minister of the First Congregational Church of Cincinnati, and then, in 1839, accepted the newly created position of Minister of the Poor in the city.[1]

A group of prominent Cincinnatians who were friends of Perkins established this new position with some financial support from the American Unitarian Association. Intended to become the main source of local charitable action, the ministry had the larger purpose of overseeing the general moral and social conditions in the city. It offered Perkins a unique opportunity to take advantage of his broad background and interests, and he plunged into the work enthusiastically. Within six months he had surveyed the entire city, developed a comprehensive picture of local conditions of poverty and vice, and defined a coherent policy to combat these problems. Although temporary relief, usually in the form of food, clothing, or fuel, was the first step toward helping the poor, the emphasis was on removing the underlying causes of suffering through educational and religious influence. As Perkins wrote in his first report: "Our aim is to *combine alms-giving with measures calculated to diminish the necessity of alms-giving; to relieve the suffering, even of the idle and vicious; but at the same time to remove the causes of suffering.*"[2]

Perkins drew the composite portrait of "Life in Cincinnati in 1840" from his personal experience as city missionary. Noting at the outset that "few of us know how our neighbors live," the author proceeded to describe the "varieties of life which now, at this hour, have their being in the city." His purpose was to acquaint Cincinnatians with the facts of life and thereby help them "put off prejudice and error, and acquire in their stead liberality and wisdom." In seven different scenes he presented a dramatic collage of the extremes of poverty and wealth, depravity and virtue, which existed in the city at this time. Perkins provides a unique contemporary picture of the moral and economic differences that distinguished the wealthy but selfish elite, the poor but honest householders, and the ambitious but anonymous newcomers in Cincinnati.

In the first scene of the story, a room twelve by eight feet, a mother and her five children, abandoned by the father, face starvation and freezing. Despite every effort, and an "honest, industrious and religious" upbringing, the family has "no money, no meat, and no bread; a little lard, a few pounds of flour, a 'drawing' or two of coffee, without milk or sugar." With no friends, and their faith in God slipping, the temptations of whiskey and prostitution seem impossible to resist. In the second scene, two women of local social prominence are lounging in a lavishly decorated room of twenty-three by eighteen feet when a woman calls at the door to collect payment for the washing she has done for them. She is turned away and accused of being a thief.

In the next two scenes a family sits down to say grace before a modest but wholesome meal. Despite an injury to the father, a carpenter who hurt himself in a fall, the family is kept together and provided for by the mother, who has gone to work. In the fifth scene an ambitious young man, new to the city, turns to whiskey in his discouragement at not being able to find work. In the sixth scene the newcomer lies drunk, cold, and hungry in the middle of the street, a soul lost to the evils of drink. And in the final scene this young man has taken up with a lawless, consumptive riverman, gambling, drinking, and planning some act of violence. The story ends at this point, with the fates of each of the characters unresolved.[3]

In this and several other stories, Perkins seemed anxious to acquaint his readers with the extremes of wealth and well-being and the extent to which these conditions divided the local society. In the midst of general prosperity and plenty, he thought, Cincinnatians should not ignore the plight of the deserted mother, the family with a disabled breadwinner, or the unemployed youth in a strange city. Moreover, they should not simply dismiss these misfortunes as the consequences of individual indifference and ignorance. Perkins's victims are all decent, moral, industrious individuals caught in circumstances they cannot control; his purpose is not so much to criticize these individuals as to call for a strong sense of community responsibility. As he wrote in his first annual report: "Every man in Cincinnati is bound to help in stopping the growth of pauperism; the man of property, because his houses and goods are endangered by it; the man of family, rich or poor, because it threatens with ruin his sons and daughters; the friend of education, because it is the deadliest foe to knowledge and labor; the Christian, because it is one of Satan's chief nets to catch souls with." Such cases should concern everyone, Perkins argued, because everyone would suffer from the poverty, corruption, and vice that would result if help were not offered.[4]

In his life and writings, Perkins dedicated himself to the improvement of the Cincinnati community. Driven by a strong paternalistic commitment to a corporate concept of society based on Christian brotherhood, Perkins was confronted daily as Minister to the Poor by the growing inequalities and divisions within the local community. For a decade he struggled with this conflict between his ideals and experience, and suffered periodic attacks of deep melancholia. In December 1849 he drowned himself in the Ohio River. In the many eulogies that followed, it is ironic that Perkins's "devotion to the best interests of society" was praised in terms of the "united" sense of loss by "every class" in the community.

Concepts of Society: Natural and Artificial Differences

When Perkins first arrived in Cincinnati in 1832 he

> found himself moving among a pleasant company of hospitable, easy, confiding, plain-spoken, cheerful friends gathered from all parts of the Union, and loosened at once by choice and promiscuous intercourse from the trammels of bigotry and conventional prejudice. He breathed for once freely, and felt with joy the blood flowing quick and warm throughout his spiritual frame. He caught, too, the buoyant hopefulness that animates a young, vigorous, and growing community, and mingled delightedly with groups of high-hearted, enterprising men, just entering on new careers, and impelled by the hope of generous service in literary, professional, or commercial life.[5]

The disparity between this roseate description of an open, invigorating society in 1832 and the harsh picture of the extremes of wealth and well-being in "Life in Cincinnati in 1840" is due in part to the different purposes of these two descriptions, in part to the difference between Perkins's initial, superficial enthusiasm and his later awareness and experience, and in part to the substantial changes that occurred in the city during these eight years. Perkins and many other Cincinnatians seemed to hold simultaneously two opposing views of the local society: one stressing "natural" or cultural relationships, the other emphasizing "artificial" or economic divisions.

The different views on natural versus artificial divisions expressed depended in large part on the particular purpose of the account and the perspective of the observer. There were a number of visitors and residents who emphasized the natural openness and informality of Cincinnati society, which was in marked contrast to that of most older, eastern cities.

A visitor in the winter of 1835 found the "total want of *caste,* a complete absence of *settishness*" in Cincinnati to be "most striking" and concluded that "society is a salad, which to relish must be mixed from a variety of ingredients." Ephraim Peabody, looking back on social life in the late 1830s, recalled:

> There had not been time as yet to form those cliques and circles which necessarily grow up in older places. Everyone stood very much on his merits. Society was open and social relationships were determined, not by the accident of relationship of property, but by personal affinities. Those came together who were attracted by similarity of taste and culture; and nothing could be more frank, hospitable, and delightful, than a society organized on that natural principle.

Social differences existed, to be sure, but they depended, according to these accounts, on the "natural principle" of "similarity of taste and culture." There was a spirit of *"entente cordiale,"* the open house was the most popular form of entertainment, and a standard of "elegant simplicity" was the rule at such occasions.[6]

At the same time, however, there were other local observers who emphasized the growing artificial divisions within the Cincinnati community, based principally on distinctions of property and occupation. In 1835 Perkins complained: "Birth and wealth are far too potent in our republic still; worth and talent too impotent. Why are the blacksmith and carpenter unfit companions for the merchant and the lawyer: Is it because they are ignorant? We fear not: for though they may be ignorant, and vicious, let them acquire wealth, and presto, the mechanic is a gentleman." James G. Birney expressed the same concern when he wrote: "Men of the most groveling minds and unworthy moral characters may take their stations as *'patricians'* after succeeding in some speculation in town-lots or government land—or in pork, or flour, or tobacco, or cotton, or sugar." Both men accepted the fact that individual differences in ability and ambition resulted in great inequalities in worldly achievement, but they criticized the increasing trend to accept the nouveau riche as gentlemen or patricians simply because of their wealth, and irrespective of their personal background or character.[7]

Implicit in these two descriptions of Cincinnati society during the 1830s is a distinction between social stratification in terms of a horizontal axis, organized according to natural cultural and moral distinctions, and social stratification in terms of a vertical axis, organized according to artificial occupational and economic divisions. Peabody, Perkins, and Birney all agreed that there were differences within the Cincinnati population along both axes, but they felt that natural differences, and not artificial ones, represented the proper basis for social distinctions. Perkins indicated his preference for horizontal distinctions of character when he expressed his "antagonism to a reverence for mere wealth or professional knowledge, unsupported by ability or worth." And Timothy Walker made the same point when he declared: "The upright man is a gentleman, no matter what his calling."[8]

As Cincinnati grew in size and complexity, cultural and economic differences within the population became increasingly articulated, and the relationship between the natural horizontal axis and the artificial vertical axis of social organization gradually changed. Before 1830, when the city's population was still relatively small and homogeneous, vertical social and economic differences had existed within a common horizontal Buckeye culture. During the 1830s, however, the cultural and economic organization of the city began to change in two fundamental ways. First, the arrival of the Yankees and Germans created a much larger and more heterogeneous cultural base. Second, the expansion and prosperity of the local economy created a more specialized and stratified occupational and economic hierarchy.

In response to the demographic pressures of rapid growth and diversity, and the failure of assimilation, the horizontal base of the population came to be redefined in moral terms, and the community restricted to the more stable, established householders. At the same time, in response to the economic changes resulting from expansion and prosperity, and the breakdown of the corporate concept of society, the vertical hierarchy came to be redefined in terms of wealth, and society opened to new groups of successful, self-made men. As the horizontal dimension of the community became more exclusive in order to maintain social order, the vertical dimension of the society became more inclusive in order to recognize individual achievement. Although the two dimensions of social organization were still closely related in 1840, the result of these changes was evident at midcentury with the emergence of a new and expanded wealthy elite composed of competing cultural groups.

With the emergence of the nouveau riche elite, the artificial or economic distinctions that Perkins had objected to superseded the natural or cultural distinctions of the earlier period as the primary criterion in the social stratification of the community. In describing the social structure of the Cincinnati community in 1840, therefore, the question is not whether the householders were stratified, but how? In order to answer this question it is necessary first to describe the important economic and occupational groupings and their particular social composition; second, to determine the relationship between economic and occupational status and the degree to which they formed a coherent, clear-cut, comprehensive class structure; and third, to consider the extent of social mobility and class consciousness. An analysis of economic and occupational stratification within the context of social mobility and class consciousness suggests that there was a clear but changing relationship between the relative horizontal position and vertical status of the householders, and that the community can be described more accurately according to a multidimensional model of a cone.

Property Ownership: Distribution of Wealth

Cincinnatians "all agreed upon one thing," a visitor remarked after a short stay in the city in 1839, "viz the acquisition of wealth." An acquisitive impulse, which seemed to infuse the entire population with a desire for economic gain, was one of the most striking characteristics of the community during this period. As a knowledgeable local resident wrote: "Whether it be called avarice, or the love of money, or the desire for gain, or the lust of wealth, or whether it be softened to the ear under the guarded terms, prudence, natural affection, diligence in business, or the conscientious improvement of time and talents—it is still *money-making* which constitutes the great business of our people—it is the use of money which controls and regulates everything." Cincinnati was, according to the prevailing view, a city of self-made men, where everyone worked and most men had something to show for it. The local booster literature claimed that "almost every man owns the house he occupies" and that "all had been the result of labor judiciously applied by a population originally poor."[9]

The favorite example of a successful self-made Cincinnatian, which local boosters and visitors cited over and over, was that of Nicholas Longworth. In 1804, at the age of twenty-one, Longworth, the son of an impoverished New Jersey Tory, arrived in Cincinnati. He took up the

Table 3.1 Number of Pieces of Property by Decile, 1838 (%)

	Owner Deciles										Total Number
	1	*2*	*3*	*4*	*5*	*6*	*7*	*8*	*9*	*10*	
One piece of property (*N* = 509)	8.0	21.8	37.6	56.3	66.3	67.4	66.7	81.1	92.9	93.0	59.0
Two pieces of property (*N* = 170)	10.2	20.7	25.9	28.7	22.1	29.1	29.8	18.9	4.8	7.0	19.7
More than two pieces of property (*N* = 184)	81.8	57.5	36.5	14.9	11.6	3.5	3.6	0	2.4	0	21.3

profession of law, but like many other men of his generation, his mind soon turned to land speculation. For defending a man accused of horse stealing, Longworth received two secondhand copper stills in payment. Since they were full, and he had no interest in selling liquor, he traded them to a tavern keeper for a thirty-three acre lot to the west of the city. At the time men thought Longworth was crazy, but this property, and other pieces acquired over the years, made him the wealthiest property owner in Cincinnati by 1840.[10]

Longworth's position as Cincinnati's largest property owner is evident in the 1838 Cincinnati Tax List, which enumerated over one hundred pieces of property that he owned, alone or in partnership, evaluated at over $115,000. This tax list also indicates the extent of property ownership in the city and the general distribution of wealth. Although it records only the assessed value of real estate within the city (which was generally considered to be undervalued) and does not include the value of personal estate (which was the main form of wealth of many citizens, particularly merchants who had capital invested in merchandise), this tax list represents better than three-quarters of the total wealth of Cincinnati.[11]

According to the 1838 Cincinnati Tax List there were 2,559 property owners who held real estate in the city worth a total of $4,935,500. These 2,559 property owners represent approximately 6% of the total population of the city, and less than a fifth of the total adult white male population. The 863 householders who were property owners represent approximately 10% of the total number of men included in the 1840 *Directory*. Clearly, despite Charles Cist's contention that Cincinnati had a larger proportion of residents who owned their homes than any other city in the United States, most Cincinnatians did not own any property at this time.[12]

The 1838 Tax List also indicates that property wealth was unequally distributed in Cincinnati. Of the total number of 2,559 property owners, the top decile, 256 owners, controlled 55.4% of the property in the city; the top half, 1,279 owners, controlled 92.1% of the property; while the lower half of the owners controlled only 7.9% of the real estate in Cincinnati. Broken down into deciles of wealth, the top 10% of the property was owned by just six taxpayers—Nicholas Longworth, the United States Bank, James Ferguson, George W. Jones, George N. Hunt, and the

William Barr Estate; the top half of the property was owned by 202 men, while the lowest 10% of the property was owned by 1,354 individuals.[13]

The distinction between the top decile, the top half, and the bottom half of the property owners is an arbitrary one, but it reflects certain basic differences in the character of the property owned by these people. Of the 1,274 property owners in the bottom five deciles, who all owned property worth less than $750, over four-fifths owned a single piece of property and less than 2% owned more than two pieces of property. This suggests that these small property owners can be characterized as homeowners. At the opposite extreme, of the 256 property owners in the top decile, who all owned property worth at least $4,220, more than four-fifths owned at least three pieces of property, and less than 10% owned but a single piece of property. This suggests that these property owners owned more than their own homes, and can be characterized as investor-speculators.

The Property Owners: A Demographic Profile

The 2,559 Cincinnati property owners in 1838 included 674 estates, companies, and other combined groups; 379 women; and 1,506 men. Only 863 of these men, however, can be positively identified in the 1840 *Directory*. Although these 863 householders make up only a third of the total group of property owners, they were quite representative, in the distribution of their wealth, of the total property-owning group.[14]

A demographic analysis of these 863 property-owning householders indicates that there was a very weak correlation (ϕ =.069; ϕ^2: .005) between property ownership and nativity but a much stronger correlation (ϕ = .344: ϕ^2: .118) between property ownership and priority. This suggests that where a Cincinnatian was born was much less important than how long he had been an adult resident of the city in determining the probability that he would own some property. Indeed, it suggests that the low proportion of property owners within the Cincinnati population during this period may be largely the result of its rapid growth and volatility and that property ownership should be considered primarily as one of the consequences of many years of residence in the city.[15]

With regard to nativity, the 863 property owners, compared to the 868 householders in the Shaffer sample, included a disproportionately large representation of native-born Americans and a disproportionately low representation of foreign-born immigrants. Although the Yankees

Table 3.2   Nativity Composition of 1838 Property Owners

Nativity Category	% of Property Owners (N = 863)	% of Householders (N = 868)	Nativity Index
Yankees	14.8	9.9	1.5
Buckeyes	61.8	49.1	1.3
Great Britain	17.0	16.7	1.0
German States	3.7	18.9	.2

were somewhat more overrepresented than the Buckeyes, all of the native-born nativity groups except the men born in Ohio and the western states had a larger proportion of property owners than householders. The most noticeable difference was among the foreign-born property owners; although the men born in Great Britain had approximately the same proportion of property owners as householders, the Germans had only one-fifth of the proportion of property owners as householders. In fact, the overrepresentation of property owners among the English-speaking majority of the Cincinnati community was largely compensated by the striking underrepresentation of property owners among the German-speaking minority in the city.

The very low proportion of German property owners in 1838 was probably due less to their nativity, however, than to their recent arrival in Cincinnati. In fact, a majority of the Zwanzigers who had been in the city for at least a decade owned property, and Cist reported that many of the German newcomers he talked to in 1840 expressed a strong desire to purchase their own home. The severe housing shortage and the high cost of city lots and construction, combined with the fact that few newcomers brought much capital with them when they came to Cincinnati, made it difficult to purchase a home until after a number of years. The general pattern for the newcomer was to board upon arrival in the city, then to move to a rented home, and then, after saving money for several years, to purchase a home. This suggests that property ownership was possible only after a Cincinnatian had been a stable, established householder for at least a few years.[16]

An analysis of the priority of the property owners confirms this impression. Of the 863 householders who owned property in 1838, the

Table 3.3   Priority of the 1838 Property Owners

	% of Property Owners (N = 863)	*% of Householders* (N = 868)	*Priority Index*
Old settler	52.8	16.4	3.2
New settler	10.4	56.3	.2

majority were old settlers and nearly a quarter had been adult residents of Cincinnati since 1817. This suggests that while there were very few newcomers or new settlers owning property in 1838, almost a third of the men who had been adult residents for at least a decade were property owners, and nearly half of those who had been in the city for more than two decades were property owners. The fact that only one out of ten Cincinnati householders in 1840 owned property must be evaluated in terms of the fact that six of these householders had been in the city for only a few years, and only two had been adult residents for at least a decade. This analysis suggests that age, stability, and experience were the most important prerequisites for property ownership.

As time passed and stability increased during the 1830s, Cincinnati property owners generally improved their economic position in the community. An analysis of the 273 householders listed as property owners in 1831 and 1838 indicates that 143, or 52.4%, had improved their decile position; 70, or 25.6%, had maintained their decile position; and only 60, or 22%, had fallen in decile position between 1831 and 1838. When the 179 old settlers who acquired property during the 1830s are added to this group, it is clear that nearly three-quarters of the 452 old settlers who owned property in 1838 had enjoyed some degree of economic success during the decade, either by acquiring property or by increasing the relative value of their estates.

Because it depended, to a large degree, on a measure of priority that most Cincinnatians did not have in 1840, property ownership is a better indication of the relative economic status of the old settlers than of the larger group of householders, most of whom were new settlers. The fact that the large majority of Cincinnatians did not own property reflects their lack of age and experience in the city more than their current economic condition. Although these householders had not yet become property owners, contemporary accounts suggest that most of them enjoyed general economic well-being. It is significant that Perkins needed to assist only one hundred "scholars at public charge." It is also significant that James S. Buckingham concluded after his visit to Cincinnati: "I doubt whether there is any city in the Union in which there is more general diffusion of competency of means, and comfort in enjoyments than Cincinnati."[17]

Occupational Composition:
The Professions, Commerce, and Manufacturing

In 1840 there were 14,544 Cincinnatians who worked in some occupation. Although the census only called for an occupational enumeration within five broad categories—professions, commerce, manufactures and trades, navigation, and agriculture—Cist noted in *Cincinnati in 1841* over one hundred different occupations, from attorney to wireworker, that he found in the city. These 14,544 workers represented 31.4% of the total Cincinnati population, the highest proportion of any of the major cities in the United States in 1840. This helps to explain why Cincinnati was often called the "workingman of cities."[18]

In 1840 there were 377 Cincinnatians engaged in some profession, and they represented less than 3% of the total work force in the city. Attorneys, physicians, teachers, and clergymen made up the large majority of this occupational group, but Cist also included the few editors, artists, architects, and engineers as professionals. These men clearly held a favorable position in the local society, as a writer admitted in an editorial on "the learned *professions*": "These are emphatically the aristocracy. Is a man a member of one of these? He is *learned*—by his diploma: a gentleman by prescription; and being both *learned and gentle* he is, at once, raised above the canaille, and becomes a member of that very respectable body, *genteel* society." The high status of the professionals is also indicated by the large number of young men who aspired to become attorneys, physicians, and clergymen at this time, creating a supply that was considerably greater than the demand.[19]

Although admission to the ranks of the professions was relatively easy—in lieu of a college education, a short apprenticeship in the offices of a recognized man prepared many of the attorneys and physicians— success was more difficult. Some capital or contacts were necessary, as well as training and skill, and for every young man who succeeded, like Timothy Walker, there were probably several, like James Taylor, who arrived in the city with great confidence and high hopes but after a few years became disgusted or defeated by the competition in the big city and departed. There were also great variations in income among the professionals: a prominent minister like Rev. S. W. Lynd of the Ninth Street Baptist Church had a reported income of $1,500 a year, and Walker noted in his diary that his business in 1838 was worth over $10,000; but Peter Zinn, an aspiring young lawyer, derived most of his $532.62 income in 1840 from newspaper work, and Taylor wrote in his diary that he could not open his own office until he raised $800. There were, consequently, two fairly distinct layers of the professional class: the successful self-supporting members who were active and influential in a variety of civic affairs; and the rest, who had a hard time earning an adequate income in their chosen occupation and establishing a reputation in the community.[20]

Because of the general lack of strict training, and the intense competition among colleagues, many attorneys and, to a lesser extent, physicians, editors, and even clergymen engaged in various activities outside their chosen profession. Land speculation was the most popular activity, but business and farming became profitable sidelines for some of these men. Politics and political offices attracted others. Among the careers attesting to such diversity were those of Daniel Drake, writer, teacher, and local booster as well as physician; of Nicholas Longworth, land speculator and horticulturist as well as attorney; and of William Burke, postmaster and Methodist minister.

In 1840 there were 2,044 men engaged in commercial activities in Cincinnati representing 14% of the total workforce. As in the professional group, the men in commerce can be divided into two distinct categories: the small group of large-scale, wholesale merchants and the much larger group of men who owned small retail stores. Here too, success and prominence depended on contacts and capital as much as on ability and training. The perils of commercial enterprise were as great as the rewards—Cist found that only 4 of the more than 400 men in commerce in 1828 were still in business in 1843—and the leading merchants were truly an aristocracy of achievement.[21]

Cincinnati's merchant princes were a small, select group who ran the large commercial houses and traded throughout the West and South-

Table 3.4   Census Occupational Categories, 1840

	N	%
Agriculture	80	.05
Commerce	2,044	14.25
Manufactures and trades	10,287	70.73
Navigation	1,756	12.57
Professions	377	2.59
Total	14,544	100.19

west. They dealt in produce, dry goods, and hardware, as well as in raw agricultural and mineral products and, indirectly, in credit. In the scope and style of their activities they differed completely from the small retail storekeepers. Success depended on connections and credit extensive enough to buy in the East and sell in the southern and western states. It depended on a thorough knowledge of merchandise and customers and an ability to make the right gambles in purchasing, pricing, and shipping goods. It was to the owners of the large wholesale commercial establishments that James Hall referred when he wrote: "It will require but little reflection to satisfy us that the resources of this country are controlled chiefly by that class which, in our peculiar phraseology, we term 'the business community.'" Together with the successful professionals and a small number of manufacturers and public officials, the merchants, according to Cist, represented "a large share of what is termed by some 'the good society of the city.'"[22]

The shopkeepers who had the small groceries, tobacco shops, taverns, hotels, and other stores where the local residents did their shopping had little in common with the merchant elite and stood in the middle ranks of the local society. They often owned a little property—their store, over which they sometimes lived—and had most of their capital invested in their merchandise. Economically they were more closely tied to their local clientele than to the outside sources of their goods or credit, and this gave them a quite limited, localistic frame of mind. Good customer relations were more important than a knowledge of national economic or political conditions, and understanding of the peculiar needs of their customers was more important than a mastery of the problems of credit or transportation. Sympathy and similarity to their neighbors was as

Table 3.5   Distribution of Work Force in Major Product-Defined Manufacturing Categories, 1840

	No. Establishments	No. Employees	Average No. Employees in Establishments	% Total Employees in Establishments with under 5 Employees	% Total Employees in Establishments with over 15 Employees
Wood products	229	1,557	6.8	23.6	19.6
Metal products	170	1,711	10.1	7.8	43.0
Clothing	272	1,445	5.3	59.1	18.7
Food products	175	1,567	8.9	20.2	77.9
Building	332	1,568	4.7	81.0	0.0
Other	426	2,799	6.6	14.5	2.1
Total	1,604	10,647	6.6	31.5	24.3

necessary as business acumen. Tied down to their stores, completely dependent on their customers, and susceptible to the slightest changes in local conditions, these shopkeepers really had more in common with the skilled mechanics and artisans in the community than with the merchant princes.[23]

In 1840, 10,287 men, or better than 70% of the total Cincinnati working force, were engaged in "manufacturing and the mechanical arts." Cist described some of the internal differences within this large occupational category in two different sections of *Cincinnati in 1841*. In a listing of the "occupations, trades, and pursuits" he encountered in taking the census, Cist enumerated more than fifty different mechanical occupations in alphabetical order. The inclusion of such occupations as basket makers, button turners, coach makers, carpet weavers, gilders, jewelers, surgical instrument makers, paper stainers, and stereotypers suggests that there were a number of highly specialized trades at this time. In a section called "Manufacturing and Industrial Products," Cist described the number of establishments, number of workers, and annual value of products for over one hundred different groups of local industries that he aggregated into thirteen general product-defined categories. These industries ranged in scale from sixty tailor shops averaging three employees each, with an average annual income of approximately $6,000, to five steamboat yards averaging over sixty employees each, and an annual income of nearly $120,000.

Despite this evidence of occupational specialization and large-scale operation in some industries, however, most Cincinnati mechanics worked as semiskilled artisans in small shops averaging less than seven employees, producing goods worth approximately $10,000 a year. Of the 1,614 establishments Cist listed in his "Manufacturing and Industrial Products" section, over half employed fewer than five men and only eighty employed more than fifteen men. Of the 10,647 men who worked in these establishments, nearly half worked in shops with from five to fifteen employees, and a quarter worked in larger shops and factories with more than fifteen employees. The food products workers were probably the most specialized and stratified: three-quarters of these men worked in large establishments averaging twenty-five employees each, and they included butchers, packers, sausage makers, soap and candle makers, and tanners and curriers. Men in the building industry were probably the least specialized and stratified: four-fifths of these men worked in small shops or crews with fewer than five employees, mostly as carpenters and masons.[24]

Within this large category of manufacturing and mechanical arts there were also a few large manufacturers: John W. Coleman in pork packing; James McCandless, an iron founder; George C. Miller, a coach maker; and Miles Greenwood, whose Eagle Foundry was one of the largest factories in the city. Some of these men, like Greenwood, started out as working mechanics but became more like merchant princes by the time they were running large-scale operations. Others, like Coleman, started out in commerce or finance, and knew little about the running of the factories, which they left to managers, concentrating instead on efficiency and profits. These men felt as much at home in the chamber of commerce as in the Ohio Mechanics Institute. In backgrounds, interests, and outlook, these manufacturers came to have more in common with the commercial and professional elite than with the majority of the local merchants.[25]

Among the working mechanics there were three different levels: the master mechanics, most of whom owned the shop or business in which they worked; the skilled journeymen, whose security rested on their expertise and the demand for their skills; and the large majority of unskilled workers, whose employment fluctuated with the uncertain conditions of production and consumption. Although this large group of mechanics—numbering over ten thousand men—differed greatly in training, income, and security, they had some sense of common identity, and a distrust of the remaining "non-productive" workers in society. They were known in the community collectively as "the bone and the sinew" of the city, a phrase that combined both the gratitude and condescension of the civic spokesmen.[26]

Occupational Classes: A Demographic and Economic Profile

In order to get a more detailed picture of the internal differences within the occupational structure of Cincinnati in 1840 it is necessary to turn from the aggregate-level data in the census to the individual-level data in the *Directory.* An analysis of the priority and nativity of the 868 householders included in the Shaffer sample, broken down into eight occupational groups, indicates that there were noticeable demographic differences among these groups. And an analysis of the 863 householders who owned some property in 1838, broken down into the same occupational groups, indicates a similar economic pattern. The marked similarities in the demographic and economic patterns among these eight occupational groups suggest that they reflect basic divisions within the occupational structure that corresponded, roughly, to occupational classes.

The following analysis of the demographic and economic differences among the eight occupational groups—professionals, merchants, manufacturers, shopkeepers, officials, mechanics, clerks, and laborers—indicates similar patterns in the distribution of old settlers and new settlers, Yankees and Germans, and property owners. The similarity of these patterns seems to reflect the existence of three distinct occupational classes: an occupational upper class (professionals, merchants, manufacturers, and officials) constituting 13.8% of the householders; an occupational middle class (shopkeepers and mechanics) constituting 56.9% of the householders; and an occupational lower class (clerks and laborers) constituting 23.4% of the householders.

An analysis of the occupational distribution of the old settlers and new settlers compared with that of the total group of householders indicates a relationship between priority and occupation. There are four occupational groups—professionals, merchants, manufacturers, and officials—in which the old settlers were considerably overrepresented and the new settlers underrepresented: these four occupational groups, constituting 13.8% of the householders, include over a quarter of the old settlers but less than a tenth of the new settlers. Conversely, there are two occupational groups—clerks and laborers—in which the new settlers are overrepresented and the old settlers underrepresented: these two occupational groups, constituting 23.4% of the householders, include over a third of the new settlers but less than a tenth of the old settlers. Finally, there was no noticeable difference in the distribution of old settlers and new settlers among the shopkeepers and mechanics: constituting 56.9% of the householders, these two occupational groups included 56.4% of the old settlers and 55.6% of the new settlers.

A similar pattern can be seen in the nativity of the householders broken down into these eight occupational groups. An analysis of the proportion of Yankees and Germans compared with the proportion of householders in each of these occupational groups indicates that the manufacturers, professionals, officials, merchants, and clerks were all

Table 3.6   Priority by Occupational Categories, 1840

Occupational Category	% of Old Settlers (N = 142)	% of Householders (N = 868)	Old Settler Index
Professional	7.7	4.2	1.8
Merchant	12.7	6.6	1.9
Manufacturer	2.8	1.4	2.0
Shopkeeper	12.0	11.2	1.1
Official	2.1	.8	2.6
Mechanic	44.4	45.7	1.0
Clerk	2.8	6.8	.4
Laborer	5.6	16.6	.3
None listed	9.1	7.0	1.3

Occupational Category	% of New Settlers (N = 142)	% of Householders (N = 868)	New Settler Index
Professional	3.6	4.2	.8
Merchant	3.2	6.6	.5
Manufacturer	.6	1.4	.4
Shopkeeper	8.4	11.2	.7
Official	0	.8	0
Mechanic	47.2	45.7	1.1
Clerk	10.5	6.8	1.6
Laborer	24.6	16.6	1.4
None listed	2.2	7.0	.3

overrepresented by Yankees and underrepresented by Germans. While these five occupational groups included a fifth of the householders, they included over a third of the Yankees but less than 5% of the Germans. Conversely, the laborers, who represented 16.6% of the householders, included only 3.5% of the Yankees but 40.9% of the Germans. Finally, the shopkeepers and mechanics were both somewhat underrepresented by the Yankees and Germans: the former group, representing 11.2% of the householders, included only 5% of the Yankees and 9.1% of the Germans; while the latter group, representing 45.7% of the householders, included 40.7% of the Yankees and 42.1% of the Germans.

This analysis of the eight occupational groups by priority and nativity

Table 3.7   Nativity by Occupational Categories, 1840

Occupational Category	% of Yankees (N = 142)	% of Householders (N = 868)	Yankee Index
Professional	8.1	4.2	2.0
Merchant	11.6	6.6	1.8
Manufacturer	3.5	1.4	2.5
Shopkeeper	5.8	11.2	.5
Official	2.3	.8	2.9
Mechanic	40.7	45.7	.9
Clerk	11.6	6.8	1.8
Laborer	3.5	16.6	.2
None listed	12.8	7.0	1.7

Occupational Category	% of Germans (N = 164)	% of Householders (N = 868)	German Index
Professional	1.2	4.2	.5
Merchant	1.2	6.6	.2
Manufacturer	0	1.4	0
Shopkeeper	9.1	11.2	.8
Official	0	.8	0
Mechanic	42.1	45.7	.9
Clerk	1.8	6.8	.3
Laborer	40.9	16.6	2.4
None listed	3.6	7.0	.5

reveals noticeable demographic differences within the Cincinnati work-force. First, the professionals, merchants, manufacturers, and officials all included a considerable overrepresentation of old settlers and Yankees and underrepresentation of Germans and new settlers. Second, of the general community the shopkeepers and mechanics seem to have been fairly representative in their priority and nativity composition. Third, the clerks and laborers both included a much higher proportion of new settlers and a lower proportion of old settlers than were present in the total group of householders, although the clerks were largely native-born Americans, particularly Yankees, while the laborers were predominantly immigrants, particularly Germans.

Table 3.8   Property Owners by Occupational Categories, 1840

Occupational Category	% of Property Owners (N = 863)	% of Householders (N = 868)	Property Ownership Index
Professional	7.7	4.2	1.8
Merchant	15.9	6.6	2.4
Manufacturer	3.1	1.4	2.2
Shopkeeper	12.1	11.2	1.1
Public official	4.3	.8	5.4
Mechanic	33.4	45.7	.7
Clerk	2.3	6.8	.3
Laborer	4.2	16.6	.2

This analysis suggests that age, length of adult residence in the city, and nativity all had some influence in determining occupation. It suggests that young men who had just arrived were likely to enter the local workforce as clerks or laborers, that the more settled and established English-speaking householders were predominantly mechanics and shopkeepers, and that the older, well-established native-born residents, particularly the Yankees, often rose to positions as professionals, merchants, manufacturers, and officials in the city by 1840. This analysis clearly demonstrates that there were demographic differences between occupational groups and suggests that, on the basis of relative priority and nativity, the eight occupational groups form three fairly distinct occupational classes: the professionals, merchants, manufacturers, and officials at the top; the clerks and laborers at the bottom; and the shopkeepers and mechanics in the middle. An analysis of the occupational distribution among the 863 householders who owned some property in 1838 clarifies this three-class occupational structure.

These 863 property owners represent approximately a tenth of the total group of householders and were characteristically the older, better established, and more successful members of the community. Since the correlation between property ownership and priority (ϕ = .344; ϕ^2 = .118) was greater than that between property ownership and occupation (ϕ = .184; ϕ^2 = .034), the probability of owning property seems to have depended more on the length of stable residence in the city than on the occupation of the householder. An analysis of the occupations

Table 3.9   Proportion of Property Owners in Occupational Categories

Occupational Category	Number of Property Owners (N = 863)	Estimated Number of Householders (N = 8,684)	% of Occupational Category Owning Property
Professional	65	360	18
Merchant	138	570	24
Manufacturer	26	120	22
Shopkeeper	106	970	11
Public official	38	70	54
Mechanic	289	3,960	7
Clerk	19	590	3
Laborer	36	1,440	3

in 1840 of these property-owning householders, therefore, is less indicative of the occupational bases for property ownership than the occupational composition of Cincinnati's older, more established, and successful householders.

The most overrepresented occupational group among the property owners was the public officials, roughly half of whom owned some property in 1838. Merchants, manufacturers, and professionals were also overrepresented, with approximately one-fifth of each occupational category owning property. Shopkeepers and mechanics included similar proportions of property owners and householders: approximately one-tenth of each occupational category owned some property in 1838. Finally, the clerks and laborers were the most underrepresented occupational groups: only 3% of each group owned property. The considerable overrepresentation among the professionals, merchants, manufacturers, and officials; the underrepresentation among the clerks and laborers; and the proportionate representation among the shopkeepers and mechanics reveals a pattern of economic differences within these eight occupational categories very similar to the demographic differences.

Turning to the relative value of the property owned by the householders in these eight occupational categories, a similar pattern emerges. The merchants, manufacturers, officials, and professionals all owned property worth somewhat more than the average, and approximately a fifth of the property owners in each occupational group were in the top decile of

Table 3.10 Median Decile of Property Owned by Occupational Groups

Occupational Category	Number	Median Decile	% "Investor-Speculators"
Professional	65	4.74	18
Merchant	138	3.94	17
Manufacturer	27	4.00	22
Shopkeeper	106	5.60	5
Public official	38	4.60	18
Mechanic	289	6.85	2
Clerk	20	6.90	0
Laborer	36	6.86	3

investor-speculators. The shopkeepers, mechanics, clerks, and laborers all owned property worth considerably less than the average, and they included very few investor-speculators. This economic disparity between the occupational classes is evident in that the upper occupational class and retired householders, who made up one-fifth of the men in the community, represented better than four-fifths of the investor-speculators.

These demographic and economic patterns suggest that there were two fairly distinct occupational classes that stood out within the Cincinnati work force in 1840: an occupational upper class, composed of professionals, merchants, manufacturers, and officials, that was distinguished by its high proportion of old settlers, Yankees, and property owners; and an occupational lower class, composed of unskilled clerks and laborers, that was distinguished by its large proportion of new settlers and German immigrants. The question remains, however, whether there were similar differences, and a consistent pattern, within the large occupational middle class, composed of the large groups of shopkeepers and mechanics, that represented the majority of the Cincinnati work force. An analysis of the patterns of priority, nativity, and property ownership among the five major product-defined categories of mechanics indicates that there were demographic and economic differences, but that they were not as marked as those differentiating occupational classes, and that they did not follow any consistent pattern. This suggests that there were internal differences within the occupational middle class, but that

Table 3.11   Demographic and Economic Differences within Mechanics

Occupational Category	No. of Mechanics	% Mechanics	Old Settlers Index (N = 65)	Yankee Index (N = 36)	German Index (N = 70)	Property Owner Index (N = 289)
Carpenter	116	29.3	1.0	1.0	.8	.7
Brick-Stone	45	11.4	1.3	1.0	1.0	1.1
Clothing	67	16.9	.4	.8	1.2	.5
Iron-Metal	86	21.7	.6	.5	1.0	.4
Food-Leather	41	10.3	1.8	1.1	1.3	.8
Paper, miscellaneous	41	10.3	1.4	1.8	.5	.3
Total	396	99.9	1.0	.9	.9	.7

Table 3.12   Manufacturing and Industrial Products, 1840

Product-Defined Category	No. of Establishments	No. of Employees	Average No. of Employees	Average Annual Value of Products
1. Wood	229	1,557	6.8	$ 9,706
2. Iron	109	1,250	11.5	15,858
3. Other metals	61	461	7.5	10,787
4. Leather	212	888	4.2	5,041
5. Hair, bristles	24	198	8.2	15,266
6. Cloth	36	359	10.0	11,421
7. Drugs, paints, chemicals	18	114	6.3	25,458
8. Earth (brick/stone)	51	301	5.9	4,672
9. Paper	47	512	10.9	14,246
10. Food	175	1,567	8.9	30,112
11. Science and fine arts	59	139	2.3	3,035
12. Buildings	332	1,568	4.7	2,871
13. Miscellaneous	261	1,733	6.6	12,294
Total	1,614	10,647		

none of the product-defined categories of mechanics within it clearly stood out from the general occupational class.

Mechanics made up approximately half of the Cincinnati work force and represented the large majority of the householders in the occupational middle class. An examination of the 396 mechanics included in the Shaffer sample indicates that, as a group, their patterns of priority, nativity, and property ownership represented those of the larger community. Constituting 45.7% of the total group of 868 householders, they included 44.4% of the old settlers, 40.7% of the Yankees, 42.1% of the Germans, and 33.4% of the property owners. When these 396 mechanics are broken down into six product-defined groups, however, certain differences emerge. Men working in food and leather industries, for example, included a higher proportion, and men working in clothing industries a smaller proportion of the old settlers than the mechanic group as a whole. Men working in brick and stone construction were somewhat overrepresented, and men working in paper products were somewhat underrepresented, compared with the total group of mechanics, among the property owners. Because these differences were not as great as those distinguishing the occupational upper and lower classes, and since these demographic and economic differences do not follow any consistent pattern, they therefore do not reflect any major divisions within the occupational group of mechanics. Important differences may well have existed within the occupational middle class, but they are not evident in the product-defined 1840 *Directory* definitions of occupations.

Society as a Cone: A Three-Dimensional Model of the Community

Although these three occupational classes represent only the most obvious divisions within the Cincinnati work force in 1840, they provide a useful framework for an analysis of the vertical structure of the community because they correspond, roughly, to the contemporary occupational distinctions, and because they include the large majority of the householders. Since contemporary accounts generally described the occupational middle class as the central stratum of the local society, and since the occupational middle class included the majority of the householders, it can be described as the baseline of the vertical structure of the community, above which stood the occupational upper class and the retired householders, and below which stood the occupational lower class. Using this basic vertical framework, approximately three-fifths of the community stood on the baseline, with a fifth above it, and a fifth below it.

This basic three-level vertical structure can be articulated more clearly by identifying the property owners within it. Wealth, according to a variety of contemporary sources, was an important determinant of social status in Cincinnati during this period. James Perkins and James Birney had both complained that wealth alone seemed to admit a man into the ranks of society, while David Shaffer, in "Rhymes to Suit the Times," simply asserted that "money, dear money's, the making of man." The fact that only a tenth of the householders owned any property in 1838 indicates that although the large majority of the community cannot be differentiated according to wealth, property ownership can be used as an important criterion for identifying the men at the top of the vertical structure.

Breaking the four basic occupational groups into two categories—the

Table 3.13   Occupational and Economic Composition of Community, 1840

Occupational Classes	Property Owners (N = 863)	Unpropertied Householders (N = 7,827)
Retired	146 (1.7%)	454 (5.2%)
Occupational upper class	267 (3.1%)	853 (9.8%)
Occupational middle class	395 (4.6%)	4,535 (52.2%)
Occupational lower class	55 (.6%)	1,985 (22.8%)

property owners and unpropertied householders—and assuming that property ownership is somewhat more important than occupational class in determining social status, it is possible to refine the basic three-level occupational structure into a four-class socioeconomic hierarchy. The unpropertied occupational middle class (52.2%) and the propertied occupational lower class (.6%) form the baseline and can be described as the middle class. Below it, the unpropertied occupational lower class (22.8%) forms the lower class. Above the middle class, the propertied occupational middle class (4.7%), the unpropertied occupational upper class (9.8%), and the unpropertied retired householders (5.2%) form the upper middle class. And at the top, the propertied occupational upper class (3.1%) and the propertied retired householders (1.7%) form the upper class. This four-class socioeconomic structure places just over half of the community in the middle class, a fifth below it in the lower class, a fifth above it in the upper middle class, and 4.8% at the top in the upper class.

The question remains how this vertical socioeconomic structure was related to the horizontal demographic field. An analysis of the most distinctive nativity groups (the Yankees and the Germans) and the major priority groups (the old settlers and the new settlers) indicates that, when broken down into these four socioeconomic classes, a definite pattern emerges. While the middle-class proportion of the community was fairly evenly distributed among these demographic groups, the upper-class and upper-middle-class proportion was concentrated among the old settlers and Yankees, while the lower-class proportion was composed largely of the new settlers and Germans. This suggests that an articulation of the vertical socioeconomic structure within the horizontal demographic field transforms the two-dimensional magnetic field model into a three-dimensional cone.

These vertical differences within the horizontal model are evident in a comparison between the class structure of the core of old settlers and that of the outer ring of new settlers. Nearly half of both priority groups were in the middle class and stood on the baseline of the vertical structure. However, of the remaining old settlers, the large majority stood above the middle-class baseline, while, of the new settlers, the majority stood above the middle-class baseline and, of the remaining new settlers, the majority stood below the middle-class baseline. Less than 5% of the old settlers but more than a quarter of the new settlers were in the lower class. Conversely, nearly half of the old settlers, but less than a fifth of the new settlers, were in the upper middle and upper classes. Finally, more than a tenth of the old settlers, but less than 1% of the new settlers, were in the upper class at the top of the vertical structure.

A comparison between the class composition of the Yankees and Germans indicates a similar pattern of vertical differences within the horizontal model. Three-quarters of the German householders were new settlers and this nativity group can be described as being concentrated along the outer rim of the community. Nearly half of the Germans were in the middle class; of the remaining group, however, the large majority stood below the middle-class baseline, in the lower class. While over two-fifths of the Germans were in the lower class, less than 7% were in the upper middle or upper classes. The Yankees were more representative in their priority of the total community, but the supposed advantages of a New England background suggest that they may be placed near the core of the magnetic field. Just a third of the Yankees were in the middle class; of the remaining group, the large majority stood above the middle-class baseline in the upper middle and upper classes. Indeed, while a sixth of the Yankees stood in the lower class, almost a third were in the upper middle class, and nearly a fifth were in the upper class.

This analysis of the relationship between the socioeconomic and demographic composition of the Cincinnati community indicates that its vertical structure was related to its horizontal distribution and that

the two-dimensional magnetic field model can be redefined more suggestively by transforming it into a three-dimensional cone. Although
the demographic and socioeconomic dimensions were not directly related and do not follow any consistent pattern, the general contours of
the model are clear. The middle class, composed of the majority of the
householders, formed a wide belt that ran fairly evenly across the baseline
of the cone. The lower class, composed of a fifth of the community, extended below this baseline, largely along the outer ring of the cone. The
upper middle class, composed of another fifth of the community, extended above the middle-class belt, largely in the central core and inner
ring. Finally, the upper class, composed of 5% of the community, formed
the apex of the cone and was concentrated in or near its central core.

After 1840 these divisions within the Cincinnati community, and the
relationship between the horizontal demographic and vertical socioeconomic dimensions, became increasingly articulated. Descriptions of
the population composition and definitions of particular groups within
it began to make explicit references to these divisions. At the same time,
in descriptions of local society there was a gradual shift in emphasis from
the horizontal demographic to the vertical socioeconomic characteristics. The older natural and moral distinctions within the population
continued to be paramount in descriptions of the newer and immigrant
residents of the city who were in the lower and middle class, but the
newer artificial distinctions of wealth and occupation became increasingly important in characterizations of the older, native-born members
of the community, particularly those in the upper and upper middle
class. While the large lower and outer portions of the cone continued to
be viewed, and described, in horizontal demographic terms, the higher
and more central sections came to be characterized primarily in vertical
socioeconomic terms. The result of this gradual shift in emphasis was to
maintain the crucial moral notion of a distinct stable community within
the larger volatile population, but to open the upper levels of society and
incorporate the nouveau riche aristocracy.

These changes are evident in the increasing interest, around midcentury, in the growing occupational divisions within the community. In a
series of editorials on "Professions and Trades" in 1852, the Cincinnati
Commercial pointed out that there was a great gap between the "pre-
eminence" of lawyers and doctors and the "low esteem" of mechanics in
local society. This had led to an unfortunate condition: "It is an almost

universal thing with us, for young men without fortune, who have obtained a liberal education, to engage in legal or medical pursuits, as presenting the most inviting career to ambition." The result was that many men without the necessary aptitude or ability glutted the professions, while there was an undersupply of talented young men learning trades. The *Commercial* admitted that "the right of the mechanical arts to a co-ordinate rank and dignity with the learned professions" was not yet recognized by the general public but asserted that, in fact, "the most wealthy—most influential—most industrious—most useful and most comfortable livers, are those who once made, or now make, mechanic's tools their companions."[27]

At the same time, there was a greater recognition of the economic differences among Cincinnatians, particularly the magnitude of the large estates of the city's wealthiest citizens. In 1844, for the first time, there was a published breakdown of the number of Cincinnati property holders at different levels of wealth. During the next twenty years, local newspapers periodically published lists of the largest taxpayers of the city, culminating with a special edition of the *Commercial* in 1865 that listed the annual income of more than nine thousand Cincinnatians. Descriptions of the Queen City during this period invariably recounted the story of Nicholas Longworth's fortune, estimated at twelve million dollars when he died in 1863, and speculated on the number of other Cincinnatians worth at least a million dollars.[28]

Beginning in 1845, local newspapers began to carry society news items about the "Upper Five Hundred of Our City." In various notes about social gatherings, marriages, divorces, and other scandals, in which the individuals were often identified only by initials, it was clear that a nouveau riche society, distinguished by its great wealth and ostentatious style, was becoming articulated at the top of the local social structure. The Burnet House Soiree, in May 1850, marking the formal opening of the world's largest and most luxurious hotel in the Queen City, was the premiere social event of this period, and local newspapers reported the names of the many members of the "Upper Fives" who were in attendance. In 1853 a *Commercial* editorial described the changes in Cincinnati society since 1835, noting the decline of "that old structure of 'old timers' . . . with a 'cod-fish' prefix, called aristocracy" and the "formation of different sets, among the intelligent, tasteful, and wealthy . . . no less refined, enlightened, or possessed with means." By midcentury, according to one knowledgeable local society, there were "four distinct circles of fashionables: first, is the real, old aristocracy; second, the monied aristocracy; third, the church aristocracy; and fourth, the school aristocracy." The fact that the latter three groups had risen to coequal status with the former was evidence of the opening of the upper levels of society: "It is much easier to get into the higher circles now than [in 1840]."[29]

During this period a new middle-class consciousness also developed. In 1841 a Working Men's Association formed in Cincinnati for the "promotion of equality of social condition." In its preamble, the association called upon all "fellow-laborers" to join together according to "the benign principle of the greatest good to the greatest number." Its grievance was basically economic, but the principal cause was identified as legislation that discriminated against labor: "Our rights are standing upon an apex of wealth instead of its base, supported and upheld in an unnatural way by bad legislation, which not only gives preference to capital over labor, but creates capital as its agency, thereby rendering the family of Industry tributary to and dependent on the family of Idleness." In order to capture political control from the nonproductive class—specifically the merchants and lawyers—the association resolved to "begin the good work of reform by placing working men in our offices of honor and trust—men who will legislate for the true interests of those who placed them there."[30]

The following year, 1842, a new Working Man's Party made good on this resolution by fielding a slate of candidates for local office. Unlike an earlier Trades Union Society, which was primarily interested in improving wages and working conditions in 1836–37, the new party focused on the general economic and political inequities within the social system and it called for all members of the "productive class" to "take *our own affairs* into our own hands." *"One interest, one destiny"* for all working men was the motto of the new movement.[31]

The new party succeeded in placing more than a dozen working men—drawn from the ranks of small manufacturers and shopkeepers, including foreign-born as well as native-born—in municipal office. Within two years, however, they shifted their political allegiance to the two established parties (dividing nearly evenly between the Whigs and Democrats), and the Working Man's Party disappeared with the return of economic prosperity. For the remaining years of the decade, workers continued to agitate for better wages and working conditions, but within the context of their specific trade rather than as members of a more broadly defined "productive class." In 1850, however, a more "united and determined effort" to represent labor emerged, again, and sixty-seven unions formed during the decade to promote their common economic interests. By this time, many of the workers in the rapidly growing and industrializing city had developed a sense of distinctive economic position and identity within the Cincinnati community.[32]

During this period, particularly during the great cholera epidemic of 1850–51, Cincinnatians also became more concerned about the large underclass that existed in the city. In 1850 the City Missionary published its seventh annual report, noting the presence of more than a thousand "grog shops," and four thousand "women lost to virtue and God" on the streets of the city. In 1851 the *Gazette* pointed to the "large *floating, unacclimated* population" in the city as a primary cause of its growing health and moral problems. Both mortality statistics following the cholera epidemic and crime statistics throughout this period emphasized the large number of outsiders and immigrants in the totals. Articles on gambling, vice, "street begging," "loafers," suicides, the theater, and "low life" filled newspaper columns in the late 1840s and early 1850s and made a clear connection between the demographic character of these people and their moral and social situation. In "A Delectable Scene," the *Commercial* described in vivid detail the "crime, vice, misery, brutality, drunkenness, a disregard for all that is human" that characterized the life of the large lower portion of the Cincinnati population.[33]

Looking at this general process from a broader perspective, Edward Mansfield described the changes in Cincinnati society between 1826 and 1876, particularly the increasing stratification of the population and its consequences:

> The great body of the people [in 1826] were mechanics, with plenty to do, generally owning their own houses, and, in fact, a well-to-do people. There will be found many improvements, much wealth and show [since then]; but beside all the art and elegance, stands gaunt poverty, events which make humanity shudder, and distress which no human power can relieve. In the midst of it all [in 1876] it is only the great middle class, which preserves the social system from decay and ruin. Cincinnati in 1826, was composed almost wholly of this class, and it was pleasant to see them, in their plain but independent houses, enjoying the fruit of their

labor. . . . It is true the city was then small, but the condition of the people was widely different. In proportion to the population, there was not one in need of [charity] where there are ten today. When I look back upon Cincinnati of 1826, and then upon Cincinnati in 1876, I find it difficult to say that being big, rich, and showy has made society better or happier.[34]

"The Ups and Downs of Society": Social Mobility

Specialization and stratification are the inevitable consequences of economic development and were inherent in the evolution of Jacksonian urban society. During a period of dynamic expansion, rapid urbanization, and growing industrialization, Americans enjoyed unprecedented opportunities for individual advancement. This was, according to many observers, the age of the self-made man, and the careers of Cincinnatians are dramatic evidence of this phenomenon of widespread mobility. The question remains, however, how extensive social mobility was and how it was related to geographical mobility. More specifically, it is necessary to consider the means by which many Cincinnatians, particularly in relation to the number who left the city after a few years, improved their socioeconomic position in the community either by moving into a higher occupational class, or a higher wealth decile, or by acquiring property.

With the transformation of the two-dimensional field model into a three-dimensional conic model, it is possible to consider this question of social mobility within a dynamic structural context. In the original two-dimensional magnetic field, there was a strong centripetal attraction toward the center of the field, reflecting a greater sense of common identity and commitment to the city that developed with increasing age and experience in the city. This magnetic attraction was strongest among the old settlers in the core, less strong among the rest of the householders, particularly the new settlers, in the middle ring, and virtually absent among the newcomers, who stood along the periphery outside the community. By bringing out the vertical socioeconomic dimension within this horizontal demographic field, the model not only adds a dimension but, more important, the thrust of this magnetic force is refined. It is now possible to consider the various patterns of movement within the cone, whether horizontal and vertical mobility are related, and to what extent the cone served as a kind of escalator, drawing Cincinnatians upward as they remained in the city over time.

In order to consider these questions about the internal dynamics of the conic model, it is necessary to place the Shaffer sample in a temporal context. Specifically, it is necessary to consider the relationship between priority (relative length of adult residence in the city before 1840) and persistence (relative length of adult residence in the city after 1840) and the occupational and economic mobility patterns of those householders who continued to live in Cincinnati for at least a decade. This requires an analysis of patterns of geographical and social mobility between 1820 and 1860, and the concomitant structural changes within the cone.

An analysis of persistence within the Cincinnati community in the years following 1840 indicates that approximately four out of ten householders moved or died within a few years, and that two more had disappeared from the city by midcentury; of the four householders who were still in Cincinnati in 1850, at least two remained through 1860. Of the 868 householders included in the Shaffer sample, there were 356 mobiles (41.0%) who did not appear in the 1843 directory, or any subsequent directory. Of the 338 stabiles (38.9%) who appeared in the 1850 directory, 225 (25.9%) also appeared in the 1860 directory and can be defined as the old-timers of the community. This means that while less than half of the householders remained in Cincinnati for a decade, over a quarter continued to live in the city for more than two decades.

These patterns of priority and persistence among the Shaffer sample of 1840 correspond, in their basic outlines, to the larger mobility patterns of Cincinnatians during the period 1820 through 1860. In each decade, approximately a fifth of the householders had been in the city for at least ten years: in 1829, 15.9% were also listed in the 1819 directory; in 1840, 16.4% were listed in the 1829 directory; in 1850, 17.3% were listed in the 1840 directory; and in 1860, 15.5% were listed in the 1850 directory. A similar, but less consistent, persistence pattern existed: of the 1819 householders, 39.2% remained through 1829; of the 1829 householders, 24.8% remained through 1840; of the 1840 householders, 23.9% remained through 1850; and of the 1850 householders, 36.2% remained through 1860. Despite the apparently higher rate of turnover between 1830 and 1850, it is clear that between two and four of every ten Cincinnatians remained in the city for at least a decade throughout the pre–Civil War period.

An analysis of the total length of adult residence in the city of the Shaffer sample indicates that there was a clear relationship between

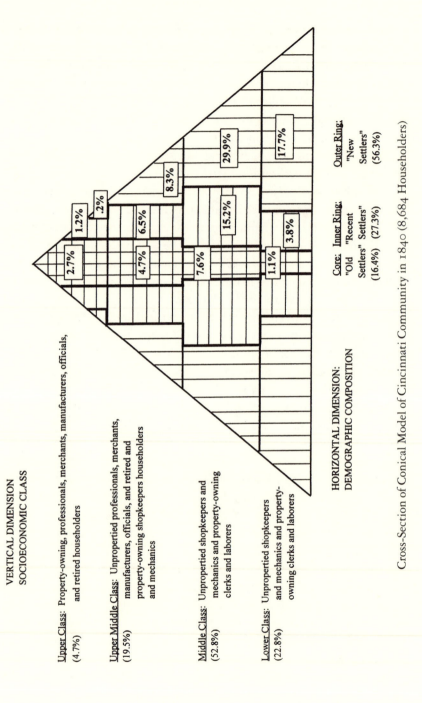

VERTICAL DIMENSION
SOCIOECONOMIC CLASS

Upper Class: Property-owning, professionals, merchants, manufacturers, officials,
(4.7%)   and retired householders

Upper Middle Class: Unpropertied professionals, merchants,
(19.5%)   manufacturers, officials, and retired and
             property-owning shopkeepers householders
             and mechanics

Middle Class: Unpropertied shopkeepers and
(52.8%)   mechanics and property-owning
             clerks and laborers

Lower Class: Unpropertied shopkeepers
(22.8%)   and mechanics and property-
             owning clerks and laborers

HORIZONTAL DIMENSION:
DEMOGRAPHIC COMPOSITION

Core: Inner Ring: Outer Ring:
"Old   "Recent   "New
Settlers"   Settlers"   Settlers"
(16.4%)   (27.3%)   (56.3%)

2.7%   1.2%   .2%

4.7%   6.5%   8.3%

7.6%   15.2%   29.9%

1.1%   3.8%   17.7%

Cross-Section of Conical Model of Cincinnati Community in 1840 (8,684 Householders) priority and persistence. Of the 142 old settlers in the Shaffer sample, only one out of ten were mobiles who died or left the city before 1843 while eight were stabiles, still in the city in 1850, and over half were old-timers who remained through 1860. Conversely, of the 489 new settlers, six out of ten were mobiles and had disappeared by 1843, only two were stabiles who remained in the city in 1850, and only one was an old-timer still in the city in 1860. This means that of the 356 mobiles, four-fifths were new settlers but only 6% were old settlers; of the 338 stabiles, approximately a third were new settlers and a third old settlers; while, of the 225 old-timers, 28.4% were new settlers and 38.6% were old settlers.

These patterns of geographical mobility suggest that within the general process of population turnover the older and most established householders were the most likely to remain in the city, while the younger and most recently arrived householders—and, by implication, particularly the newcomers—were the most likely to leave within a few years. This indicates a magnetic attraction within the cone and, to a lesser extent, within the middle ring: it held a majority of the old settlers for at least a decade, and approximately half of the householders who had been in Cincinnati since 1835, but only a fifth of the large group of new settlers. The fact that a large proportion of new settlers—and, by implication, newcomers—left the city within a few years of their arrival suggests that, in contrast to the centripetal attraction in the center of the cone, there was a centrifugal repulsion along the outer portion of the cone and the periphery.

A social analysis of the 356 mobiles and 225 old-timers indicates that they were concentrated in very different areas within the cone in 1840. Nearly a third of the mobiles were Germans; only 6 of them owned any property in 1838; and only 10.1% were in the occupational upper class. This means that in 1840 none of the upper-class old settlers were mobiles, less than one out of ten of the upper- and upper-middle-class householders who were not new settlers were mobiles, but that over half of the middle-class new settlers, and nearly two-thirds of the lower-class new settlers left the community, or died, by 1843. The mobiles clearly left from the lower and outer portion of the cone.

Conversely, the 225 old-timers who remained in Cincinnati through 1860 were predominantly located in the higher and inner portion of the cone in 1840. Nearly a third of these old-timers were in the upper or upper middle class; only a sixth were in the lower class. Of the 60 old-timers who had been in Cincinnati before 1830, a sixth were in the upper-class core area of the cone, and over half were in the core area above the middle-class baseline. Of the 68 old-timers who appeared in no directory before 1840, two-thirds were in the middle class, with the rest nearly equally distributed above and below this baseline. This means that over half of the upper-class old settlers remained in the city through 1860, that almost half of the upper- and upper-middle-class householders who were not new settlers were old-timers, but that only a sixth of the middle-class new settlers, and less than a tenth of the lower-class new settlers, lived in Cincinnati for another two decades after 1840.

The question remains whether the more settled established householders generally changed occupations, acquired property, and improved their socioeconomic position during their extended residence in Cincinnati. An analysis of the occupational and economic mobility patterns of 210 men whose names appear on both the 1817 and 1838 tax lists, and of the 225 old-timers who remained in the city between 1840 and 1860, indicates a fairly consistent pattern. Occupationally, most of these men changed their occupational designations—indicating either real changes in jobs and trades or simply changes in directory definitions of occupations—but not their occupational category or class during these twenty-year periods; of those who did change their occupational classification, a majority improved their occupational status. Economically, however, many of these men acquired property or increased the relative value of their real estate. This suggests that economic mobility was more common than occupational mobility and that, for many Cincinnatians, an extended residence in the city resulted in some upward socioeconomic mobility.

Of the 210 old settlers whose names appear on the 1817 tax list, 167 were listed with occupations in both the 1819 and 1840 city directories. During the two decades following 1819, the majority of these old settlers changed their occupational designations in the directories at least once: 52 (31.1%) had the same occupation throughout the period; 56 (33.5%) changed occupations once; 31 (18.5%) changed occupations twice; and 28 (16.5%) changed occupations three or more times. Of these 167 old settlers, however, 97 (58.0%) remained in the same occupational category throughout this twenty-one-year period while 48 (28.7%) moved into a higher occupational category and 22 (13.3%)

moved into a lower occupational category. Of the 58 (34.7%) old settlers who changed occupational class in the process, 40 (68.9%) moved into a higher class while 18 (31.1%) fell into a lower class.

A similar pattern of prevalent changes in occupational designation but predominant stability in occupational category and class is evident among the 225 old-timers who remained in Cincinnati between 1840 and 1860. Of these, only 80 (35.5%) were listed with the same occupational designation between 1840 and 1860; 96 (42.6%) changed occupational designation once; 44 (19.5%) changed occupational designation twice; and 5 (2.2%) changed occupational designation three or more times. The majority of these stable, established householders did not improve their occupational status in the process; 138 (61.3%) old-timers did not change occupational category, 71 (31.5%) moved into a higher occupational category, while only 16 (7.1%) moved into a lower occupational category. Of the 76 old-timers who changed occupational class, 65 (85.6%) moved into a higher class while 11 (14.4%) moved into a lower class.

A very different pattern emerges from an analysis of the economic mobility of these 225 old settlers during their extended residence in Cincinnati. In both cases, the majority of the men who were property owners throughout the period improved their relative decile position, and a substantial group acquired property in the process. Of the 210 old settlers whose names appear on both the 1817 and 1838 tax lists, 130 were originally listed as property owners and 80 were listed as single men without property. Of the 130 property owners, 86 (66.1%) improved their decile position, 18 (13.8%) remained in the same decile position, and 26 (30.0%) fell into a lower decile. If the 80 unpropertied single young men are included in the analysis, over three-quarters of the old settlers improved their economic situation between 1817 and 1838. Of the 225 old-timers who remained in Cincinnati between 1840 and 1860, 148 could be found in the 1860 census. Of these 148 old-timers, 33 were property owners in 1838: 20 (60.6%) rose into a higher decile, 3 (9.0%) remained in the same decile, and 10 (30.3%) fell into a lower decile in the process. If the 75 old-timers who had acquired some property between 1840 and 1860 are included in the analysis, 64.1% of the total group improved their economic position in Cincinnati during this period.

This analysis of the mobility patterns of Cincinnatians between 1820 and 1860 suggests two important conclusions. First, the high degree of internal population turnover and the fact that only a minority of house-holders remained in the city for at least a decade suggest that the magnetic attraction within the cone had only a limited effect: that, in contrast to a centripetal force drawing men in the inner and upper portions of the cone toward the center, there was also a centrifugal force pulling men in the outer and lower portions of the cone away from the community. Second, the general pattern of occupational class stability, despite the high rate of occupational changes and economic improvement, particularly in the acquisition of property, suggests that, for the stable, established minority of householders, there was an escalator effect within the cone, drawing men upward into higher socioeconomic classes over time. These two conclusions, and the predominance of economic over occupational mobility, are dramatically illustrated in a series of articles that Cist wrote during this period.

In *Cincinnati in 1841* Cist included a section entitled "Reverses in Fortunes" in which he described some dramatic cases of "the ups and downs of society." Instances of great success and wealth were widely publicized, and did not need to be repeated, Cist noted, but the cases of failure and degeneration were usually overlooked. He found a woman who was the daughter of one of the leading clergymen in Philadelphia and the niece of a New York congressman who was working as a public prostitute in Cincinnati, a woman "whom no remonstrances can rouse, nor recollections shame." He met a former friend from Pittsburgh who once owned $50,000 worth of real estate but had degenerated into a hopeless drunkard and vagabond. And he described the story of an immigrant, the proprietor of a large foundry in Scotland, who was working as a common day laborer in the iron works in Cincinnati in 1840. "It is only by inquiry or recorded history," Cist concluded, "that we are called to contrast the affluence or the dignity of the past, with the destitutions or insignificance of the present."[35]

During the subsequent decade Cist made a comprehensive study of the career patterns of Cincinnatians, particularly those who had been residents of the community since his arrival in 1827. Stories of spectacular success, especially in cases of special obstacles or unappreciated talent, delighted Cist. A boy named Miles Greenwood, who had sold apples for his family's only income in the early 1820s, was now a "heavy business-man" and bank director. There was a man who had exhibited a monkey through the city streets for a living in 1837 who owned $30,000 worth of real estate ten years later. And there was a man who made a fortune of $50,000 between 1830 and 1837, lost it, made another fortune of $100,000 by 1841, lost it, too, and was now working on his third fortune, worth at least $20,000 in 1847. For Cist these stories represented the "romance" in the "realities of human life." On balance, however, he was more impressed with the uncertainties and lack of dramatic success demonstrated in the careers of most of the Cincinnatians he studied. "A few acquire the object of their pursuit," he concluded, but "the mass sink into obscurity and insignificance."[36]

In 1847 Cist published "Mercantile Life," an article in which he described the careers of some of Cincinnati's merchants during the last two decades. The article, based on the experiences of over four hundred men who were in business in the city in 1827, included the following examples:

No. 1. Broke, afterwards resumed business, has since left Cincinnati.
No. 2. Broke, resides now in Indiana.
No. 3. Broke, and now engages in collecting accounts.
No. 4. Died.
No. 5. Now Captain of a Steamboat.
No. 6. Left merchandising to put up pork, which business he also quit in time to save his bacon—independent in circumstances.
No. 7. Dead.
No. 8. Broke, resides now in St. Louis.
No. 9. A firm, one of the partners dies, the other out of business, both insolvent.
No. 10. Partners, both died.
No. 11. Partners, broke, one now a bookkeeper, the other dead.
No. 12. Became embarrassed and swallowed poison.
No. 13. A firm, broke.
No. 14. A firm, broke, one of the partners died a common sort, the other left the city.
No. 15. A firm, broke and left the city.
No. 16. A firm, all its members out of business.
No. 17. A firm, senior partner dead.

No. 18. A firm, senior partner dead, junior resides in Toledo.

No. 19. Is now a clerk, and left Cincinnati after becoming intemperate.

No. 20. A firm, two of the partners dead, one of whom died intemperate, the other is now engaged in other business.

No. 21. A firm, senior partner died intemperate, junior now a pastor of a Presbyterian Church.

No. 22. Died of Madeira wine.

No. 23. do

No. 24. A firm, broke, one of the partners dead, the other now in business on Pearl Street.

No. 25. A firm, junior partner in business on Pearl Street.

No. 26. A firm, broke, one of the partners now in other business, one removed to New York, and the third a clerk.

No. 27. Broke, and drowned himself in the Ohio River.

No. 28. Broke, resides in Baltimore.

No. 29. Removed to Baltimore.

No. 30. A firm, senior partner dead, the other partners dealing in real estate.

No. 31. Out of business, having broke three times.

No. 32. Broke, now dealing in flour.

No. 33. Died of Cholera.

No. 34. A firm, senior partner dead, junior gone to New Orleans.

No. 35. Broke, removed to New Orleans.

No. 36. Broke, removed to Illinois.

No. 37. Broke, removed to Missouri.

Cist concluded his list of examples with the observation: "I know of but five now in business who were so twenty years since. Such is mercantile success." The fact that the large majority of these merchants either moved from Cincinnati or died during this period is a reflection of the high rate of geographical mobility, even among the more established members of the business community.[37]

In 1852 Cist published "The Way to Wealth," which complemented "Mercantile Life" by presenting a similar list of individuals who had succeeded dramatically during the same period. Here, too, he cited his examples by number:

No. 1.   A carpenter, twenty years ago, bought property with the avails of his industry; one of the richest men in the city.

No. 2.   A carpenter, ten years ago did not own a house in the city, now worth thirty thousand dollars.

No. 3.   A tinner, one of the wealthiest men in Cincinnati.

No. 4.   A tanner and currier, began without a dollar, independently rich.

No. 5.   A tallow chandler, do.

No. 6.   A tobacconist, a large property holder in and adjacent to Cincinnati.

No. 7.   A tanner, a large property holder.

No. 8.   A bricklayer, died a few weeks since, owning property extensively.

No. 9.   A blacksmith, now extremely rich.

No. 10.   A turner, changed his business and now proprietor of a large foundry, very rich.

No. 11.   A printer, now a large property holder.

No. 12.   A carpenter, so poor in 1828, that with his wife and five children he occupied a garret as a residence, now worth fifty thousand dollars.

No. 13.   A tin and copper smith, independent in worldly circumstances.

No. 14.   A painter, owns three or four fine dwelling houses.

No. 15.   A firm in the foundry business, extremely wealthy, made all they are worth in less than twelve years.

No. 16.   A machinist in prosperous circumstances.

No. 17.   A foundry proprietor, one of the most extensive in the city, made all he is worth by industry, and without capital.

Cist's conclusion from this evidence was that "mechanical employment, in the long run, leads men generally to independence, if not riches." The evidence, however, suggests that shrewd property investment was one of the most effective roads to success in Cincinnati during the mid-nineteenth century.[38]

Together, this evidence of a subordinate pattern of socioeconomic mobility within a dominant pattern of geographical mobility conforms to the prevailing "corporate" concept of an organic society that many Cincinnatians still shared at midcentury. This corporate concept of society argued that "society is a unit. It has various organs, each dependent on the others, and no one can advance alone. . . . No class no individual is independent, society is bound together by the necessities and common interests of all its members." According to this view of society, all members of society are bound together in various unequal but interdependent relationships within an organic community. This community is crosscut by inevitable social and economic divisions, but they are not impermeable: "For the good of the community there must be proprietors as well as workingmen. Each is dependent on the other. By hard work, however, the hired hand has every chance in this country to become the hirer. . . . There must be poor and there must be rich, yet one is dependent on the other for the blessings of social life, and one is as good as the other in any and all senses, provided he behaves well."[39]

Rather than developing "exclusive interests" as members of competing classes, Cincinnatians were encouraged to allow the natural process of "elevation" to operate within the organic social context. In a series of editorials attacking the Working Men's Movement, Edward Mansfield declared: "No man can pull himself up by pulling down another. They will both tumble down together." Elsewhere, in an editorial praising a new newspaper the *Elevator,* which encouraged the "*elevation* not the leveling of different classes of society," Mansfield stated: "There are laws of social life as there are in the physical world. . . . Mankind *can* and *will be elevated.* But they can never be leveled or equalized. Perpetual motion will be found out much sooner than social equality of mankind." Mansfield's argument reflected a corporate concept of society very much like that of Perkins: although social and economic differences were acknowledged, there was a belief that with time and experience, and through sustained hard work, upward mobility was possible in an orderly, but open, evolving society.[40]

Elam Potter Langdon

James H. Perkins

Timothy Walker

Ormsby M. Mitchel

Charles Cist

Jacob Burnet

Robert Buchanan

Nicholas Longworth

4

Participation and Power: Leadership

All classes are beginning to appreciate, and in accordance with the
institutions of our country, to reward true merit by placing in responsible public stations the men who possess it, whether they be
found in the hamlet or the palace.
— *CINCINNATI GAZETTE,* JANUARY 19, 1840

The Cincinnati Observatory Story

On a cold wet morning in November 1843, Jacob Burnet led the officers
of the Cincinnati Astronomical Society and a large procession of their
distinguished members and guests through the streets of the city to an
eastern hilltop, where they laid the cornerstone for a new observatory.
After more than eighteen months of concerted work under the direction
of Burnet, its president, and Professor Ormsby M. Mitchel, its astronomer, the Cincinnati Astronomical Society had raised the funds necessary to purchase and house the largest refracting telescope in the Western
world. Already renowned for its spectacular growth and material success,
Cincinnati would now become the center for astronomical study in the
United States.[1]

The dedication of the Cincinnati Observatory was also significant in
another, more fundamental, respect. It marked the culmination of one of
the community's most ambitious and successful projects of public and
private improvement during the pre–Civil War period. It represented
the opening of another local institution developed and supported by
Cincinnatians through the means of a voluntary association. The story of
the formation of the Cincinnati Astronomical Society and the building of
the observatory provides a good example of the central role of voluntary

associations in community life, and the way Cincinnatians worked together to improve themselves and their community.[2]

The idea of building a great observatory in the Queen City grew out of a series of public lectures on the recent discoveries and theories of modern astronomy that Mitchel, professor of mathematics and astronomy at the Cincinnati College, delivered in the spring of 1842. The great popular success of the lecture series—which had to be moved to the city's largest church to accommodate an audience reported to number nearly two thousand—aroused widespread interest in astronomy and encouraged Mitchel to pursue his dream of establishing a large modern observatory in Cincinnati. After talking with several prominent citizens about the project, Mitchel called a meeting to organize the Cincinnati Astronomical Society.

A small group of community leaders who were interested in the observatory project—including Jacob Burnet, James H. Perkins, Edward Mansfield, and George Graham—met in May 1842, formed the Cincinnati Astronomical Society, named themselves as the board of directors, and then elected Jacob Burnet as president. They decided to finance the project by selling stock, at $25 a share, in the community, with the shareholders forming the membership of the society. Mitchel estimated the total cost of the purchase of a telescope and the building of the observatory would be $7,500, which meant that 300 shares would have to be sold. During the next few weeks he visited 1,200 individuals, of "all classes," to solicit money or pledges; by early June the necessary amount had been subscribed, mostly in single shares, and Mitchel set out for Europe to purchase the telescope.[3]

Contemporary accounts suggest several different interpretations of how and by whom the project was completed. According to the popular version, the Cincinnati Observatory was "the only one in the world constructed and put into operation by the people—the masses." It was public enthusiasm for astronomy, growing out of Mitchel's lectures, that provided the initial impetus for the project. Mass support—from a broad cross-section of butchers and bankers, plasterers and physicians, mechanics and merchants—provided the necessary funds to buy the telescope and begin construction of the observatory. Later, when funds ran out, many citizens contributed time, labor, and building materials to complete the project. With the opening of the observatory, the grand telescope was open to anyone who wanted to take a look at the heavens.

And Mitchel, as he often pointed out, became the first democratically elected astronomer in history.[4]

Mitchel's personal account of the construction of the telescope offers a somewhat different interpretation, however. After a short period of public enthusiasm, the community lost interest in the project and many stockholders refused to honor their pledges. In order to raise the original $7,500, Mitchel had to dun the recalcitrant stockholders, sometimes a dozen times without success, for over a month. When the building costs exceeded his original estimate and work fell behind schedule, Mitchel had to take over supervision of the construction and even do some of the actual work himself. Throughout the project, Mitchel and the original board of directors dictated the affairs of the Cincinnati Astronomical Society. Looking back on the experience, Mitchel pointed to Nicholas Longworth, who donated the land on which the observatory was built, and a handful of wealthy members, who contributed the $3,000 necessary to meet additional expenses, as his main supporters in the enterprise.[5]

Both versions of the observatory story are exaggerated, reflecting, in the popular account, the prevailing democratic assumptions of the period, and, in Mitchel's account, personal frustration and vanity. Charles Cist, who was an active supporter of the project, offered a more balanced account: "It was an example of what may be accomplished by the public spirit of a community when its energies are stimulated into activity by the enthusiasm, intelligence, vigor, and perseverance of any one man of competent ability to direct it to a successful issue." Cist's version suggests that the Cincinnati Observatory was in fact the product of the combined efforts of an aroused public and responsible leadership. Mitchel provided the idea of an observatory and directed the entire project to its successful completion. The public supported the enterprise with its initial enthusiasm and much of the needed funds and labor. A small group of wealthy community leaders gave money, time, and advice in the administration of the society. The observatory story, according to Cist, demonstrated the efficacy of cooperation and strong civic spirit.[6]

Voluntary Associations: Character and Function

In 1840 Cincinnati had a number of different voluntary associations through which interested citizens became involved in a broad range of community activities. Some were formal, permanent institutions, like banks, libraries, and fraternal lodges; others were more informal and ephemeral activities, like political rallies, fund-raising dinners, and petitions for reform legislation. Some associations, such as the volunteer fire companies, had a clearly defined, ongoing purpose that concerned most residents of the community; other associations, such as the Society for the Promotion of Useful Knowledge, had a specific, esoteric purpose of interest to only a small, select number of residents. Many associations were made up largely of men with very similar interests and backgrounds: the Friends of the South who met to improve commercial relations with the southern states were mostly large-scale merchants; the Admirers of the Fine Arts, who joined together to purchase a statue, were wealthy, socially prominent citizens with an aesthetic inclination. But other associations had a more diversified composition: the members of the ward vigilance committees of each party came from a variety of backgrounds and shared only an interest in local politics and the desire to win elections; the sponsors of the Cincinnati Fuel Oil Company included a large number of residents with a common desire to establish lower and more consistent fuel oil prices.[7]

The motives that prompted associational activity differed with each individual. For some, associations offered an opportunity to get together with old friends and to meet new ones; for others, associations provided a chance to feel part of the larger community in which they lived, and to take the first step in having a say in its affairs. Associations made it possible for people with a utilitarian or altruistic purpose to accomplish together what could not be attempted alone. And for those with some personal ambition or sense of civic responsibility, associations represented the means through which influence and energy could be transmitted to the broader community. Cutting across the established ties of family, friendship, and work, voluntary associations offered interested citizens an opportunity for new and broader contacts, communication, and cooperation in a rapidly expanding city.

Cincinnatians appreciated the importance of these associations. Local booster literature and newspapers always listed community associations and often reported their activities, including, in some instances, detailed descriptions of the issues and individuals involved. Cincinnati writers and orators usually mentioned the prominent role of associations in the development of the city and attributed much of its success to their efforts. And obituaries commonly cited the associations in which the deceased had been active, implying that such activity, along with family life and a business career, were the criteria by which a man was finally judged. Associations were clearly recognized as an integral part of the community: they played a central role in promoting the diverse activities of Cincinnatians.

The unique role of associations in America was the subject of Perkins's essay "Associations: A Vital Form of Social Action," in which he argued that they replaced the aristocratic institutions of the old world. With the triumph of democracy, Perkins began, Americans had to "give up classes, and corporate bodies of every kind, and come to simple direct individualism." The "prevailing antagonism to all corporations, all privileged bodies, and castes of every kind," created "a curious condition of things; no recognized order, and no church, and yet much of the same desire for action in masses which had always existed, and must exist until ignorance and vice cease from the earth." As a result of this vacuum there had been the "production of voluntary associations to an immense extent," which, Perkins concluded, were "the true LIVING MODE OF ACTION on the part of society in America."[8]

Timothy Walker, too, was interested in the phenomenon of associational activity, which he felt was critical to the effective organization of the "social dispositions" of a community. He described the associative process in the following way: "Some individual conceives a high or useful enterprise. He has not the means to execute it himself; but he proposes it to those around him, and they, if it be reasonable, concur in his views. The flame once kindled spreads like a fire in the forest. A society is formed, and funds begin to accumulate. . . . This drop of charity grows into a stream, the stream swells into a river, and the river pours its accumulated treasures into an ocean of social benevolence." Most associations were utilitarian, Walker noted, and the implicit assumption in every group was, "We mean to receive as much as we give, and we ask others to join us on that principle." In a larger sense, however, the effect of associations was integrative. Without associations, "only a bare and miserable skeleton of social existence would remain"; but with them, society enjoyed the benefits of a "noble and expansive feeling which identifies self with community."[9]

As Perkins and Walker indicate, voluntary associations represented an important local institution that played a central role in the organization and operation of community life. Although the motives that prompted individuals to become active varied, voluntary associations provided everyone with a chance to become involved in local affairs. Although every association had a distinctive form, character, and purpose, they all prompted communication and cooperation among the citizens of the community. In many different particular contexts, therefore, associational activity drew individuals together and developed a sense of larger group identity and purpose. Voluntary associations formed a loose network within the community that served as the institutional framework for citizen participation and power.

The Associational Network: Formal and Informal Organizations

As mentioned above, most of the voluntary associations in Cincinnati in 1840 can be divided into two broad groups: permanent, formal organizations such as banks, educational institutions, masonic lodges, and fire companies; and the ephemeral, informal meetings, committees, and other groups, which met for some immediate purpose. Although this distinction is arbitrary in some cases—some formal permanent organizations met irregularly and their membership changed frequently—most associations can be classified in one or the other group.

Formal, permanent organizations generally had regularly elected officers, standard requirements for membership, and some well-defined ongoing purpose. Such groups included the Cincinnati Savings Institution, the city council, the chamber of commerce, the Society for the Promotion of Useful Knowledge, the Young Men's Bible Society, the Nova Cesarea Harmony Masonic Lodge, and the Washington Fire Company. These organizations were listed in Cist's *Cincinnati in 1841* and Shaffer's *Directory for 1840* with the names of their officers.

One of the earliest, largest, and most important formal organizations in Cincinnati was the volunteer fire department. In 1802, the year that Cincinnati received its village charter, an ordinance was passed charging every householder with the purchase of a two-and-a-half gallon blackjack leather bucket and service any time the cry "fire" was called. In 1810 the Washington Company formed, purchased an engine and other equipment, and accepted responsibility for answering any fire alarm. By

Table 4.1   Formal Organizations, 1840

General Category	No. of Organizations	No. of Officers
Banks and insurance companies	16	160
Benevolent institutions	18	60
Municipal government	4	129
Fraternal	15	42
Fire companies	12	58
Total	65	449

1819 there were three such companies; a decade later the number had increased to ten; and by 1840 twenty-five fire companies served the burgeoning city.

During the early years of the city, nearly every able-bodied man in the community belonged to a fire company. Members took great pride in their companies, which purchased expensive equipment and outfitted themselves in extravagant uniforms. Most companies had a fire house, which became a social center for the men and children of the area. Competing against the other companies of the city in the elegance of their equipment and uniforms, as well as in their performances fighting fires, the volunteer fire companies were a strong source of local pride and cohesion. During the first half of the nineteenth century, the volunteer fire companies were the largest and most popular formal organizations in Cincinnati.[10]

Less open in their membership, but no less popular or important to their members, were the numerous fraternal lodges. In 1794, just five years after the founding of Cincinnati, the Nova Cesarea Harmony Lodge was organized by some of the leading citizens of the small community. During the following years many prominent residents were associated with the Lodge; by 1840, the membership and activities of most fraternal organizations were made up primarily of mechanics and petty shopkeepers, who had a desire for some good fellowship and some romance and mystery in their lives. The popularity of fraternal groups during this period reflected the increasing population and impersonality of the city, and the desire among many citizens for a small, stable center of activity and friendship.[11]

Table 4.2   Informal Groups, 1840

General Category	No. of Meetings	No. of Participants
Political	92	775
Philanthropic	12	302
Mutual aid	3	114
Slavery issue	9	203
Patrons of the arts	3	86
Friends of the South	4	47
Professional	11	349
Banking issue	7	184
Total	141	2,060

A highly selective membership and an ambitious, high-minded purpose characterized the Society for the Promotion of Useful Knowledge. Founded in 1840 by a group of 159 prominent, education-minded citizens as an indirect descendant of the College of Teachers, this organization meant to improve its members by *"mutual instruction"* in *"regular courses of popular lectures."* The entire body of human knowledge was divided into fourteen separate areas, and members selected one area, which they studied in an intensive weekly seminar for an extended period of time. Also, the society gave regular lectures, open to the public, on a variety of subjects of more general interest. Thus the members improved themselves, made their knowledge and resources available to the larger community, and hoped to encourage "a general taste for moral, intellectual, and social progress."[12]

The more informal, ephemeral groups were generally organized for a single immediate purpose, had appointed or popularly elected officers for the duration of their existence, and were usually open to any interested citizens. Sometimes the informal groups were meetings, such as a political ward meeting at the local fire house to elect delegates or candidates, a meeting at the College Hall to promote free banking, or a banquet honoring a distinguished citizen or visitor. Other groups were informal committees formed to sponsor some project, such as the candidacy of a local politician; or to thank a visiting artist or actor; or to promote some particular business, cultural, or philanthropic enterprise. These meetings and committees were generally reported in the local newspapers, with a description of their business and a list of the officers and participants.

As might be expected, the majority of these informal groups convened at political meetings and committees. Every year both parties held numerous meetings throughout the city to nominate delegates and candidates, arouse the loyal into action, and try to win over the members of the opposition. Like all political affairs of the period, there was always a group of distinguished party leaders on the platform who directed the meeting and delivered impassioned speeches, perhaps a few honored guests or featured speakers, and the assembled citizens who made up the audience. During the 1840 campaign, according to Mansfield, such meetings were held almost every night during the weeks preceding the election. Then, on one of the last evenings of the campaign, each party held a grand rally, the Democrats at the courthouse, the Whigs at the Fifth Street market:

> The Democrats rallied their forces at the public landing at the river, and marched from there to the courthouse. I was sitting in my mother's, on Third Street, near Broadway, when I heard huzzas and the heavy tramp of feet going up Broadway. I rushed out to see what was the matter. It was the Democratic procession, marching by platoons to the courthouse. The whole street seemed to be dark with them. Each man seemed to carry a club, which he struck against the ground, and hurraed for Van Buren. Many were German and Irish. "Hurra for Van Buren," was constantly heard in the deep guttural voices, which seemed to be so earnest and determined. I had never before seen so large a procession moving that way, and felt alarmed for the result. Going immediately to the Fifth Street market, I was undeceived; there I saw the space filled with thousands of people. Four or five different speaker's stands were erected, and the most popular orators of the day were speaking to the multitude in animated terms.[13]

Most political meetings were much smaller. These meetings, often held at the local fire house or in a large church or public hall, were the most common and widely attended associational activities in the community. For many residents, attendance at such a meeting was the result of curiosity or a minimal sense of party responsibility; for the ambitious aspiring politician, however, such meetings and committees served as a ladder to positions of power or candidacy. In addition, there were numerous small meetings, dinners, committees, and other gatherings of citywide groups that directed party policy, honored the faithful and successful, and demonstrated who was supporting which party in elections. These groups generally consisted of the most active and influential ward politicians and can be described as a citywide leadership group. Although there was an important difference between the men who indicated their support of the party by simply attending a mass rally and a ward delegate or member of the party's central committee, all of these men who demonstrated a minimum degree of interest and identification with the Whig or Democratic parties are to be considered the central participants in the community.

The Activists: A Social Analysis

Of the 8,684 male householders included in Shaffer's *Directory for 1840,* 1,050 were mentioned at least once in some newspaper report of a local meeting, committee, or other informal group, and 396 were identified as officers of formal organizations listed in the city directory or guidebook. Together, the 1,194 activists who participated or held power in Cincinnati during the three year period 1839–42 represent 13.7% of the men included in the 1840 directory. Despite the large number and wide variety of voluntary associations in the city at this time, associational activity was clearly restricted to a small proportion of the men of the community. More important, an analysis of the social composition of these 1,194 activists indicates that they stood out within the larger community as a distinctively stable, select, and successful minority.

In regard to priority, the activists had been adult residents of Cincinnati for considerably longer than the total group of householders: while over half of the sample were new settlers who appeared in no directory before 1840, this is true for only a quarter of the activists; conversely, while less than a fifth of the sample were old settlers whose names appeared in the 1829 directory, this is true for over a third of the activists. This suggests that, within an adult white male population marked by its relative youth and lack of established roots in the city, the activists were distinguished as a relatively mature, experienced, and stable minority.[14]

In regard to nativity, the activist group included a somewhat larger proportion of native-born Americans, particularly those from New England, and a smaller proportion of foreign-born residents, particularly

Table 4.3   Social Composition of the Activists, 1840

	% of Activists (1,194)	% of Shaffer Sample (868)	% "Activists" / % Sample
Priority			
Old settler	49.6	16.4	3.0
New settler	20.8	56.3	.3
Nativity			
Yankee	15.6	9.9	1.57
Buckeye	62.5	49.1	1.27
Great Britain	12.7	16.7	.76
Occupation			
Upper	40.8	13.0	2.9
Middle	42.8	56.9	.8
Lower	8.6	23.4	.4
Retired	7.8	6.7	1.2
Wealth			
Property holder	35.3	10.9	3.21

recent German immigrants, than the general Cincinnati population of 1840. The socially prominent Yankees were quite active in local voluntary associations, while the newly arrived Germans, who were often isolated from the general English-speaking community by their foreign language and culture, had not yet become involved in the associational network by 1840.

In occupational composition, the activist group included a disproportionately large number of professionals and merchants, and a relatively small proportion of mechanics and laborers. The upper occupational class (professionals, merchants, manufacturers, and officials) constituted only 13.8% of the sample but 42.6% of the activists. In the middle occupational class, shopkeepers represented 11.2% of the sample and 13.9% of the activists but the mechanics, who constituted 45.7% of the sample, included only 28.9% of the activist group. Within the lower occupational class, clerks, who represented 6.8% of the sample, made up 7.5% of the activists, but laborers, who represented 16.6% of the sample, included only 1.1% of the activists. Associational activity was clearly correlated with higher occupational status, with men in professional, managerial, and commercial positions constituting nearly two-thirds of the total group of activists.

There was also a strong relationship between associational activity and property holding. Only a tenth of the male householders, but better than a third of the activists, owned some real estate in Cincinnati in 1838. There was also a strong relationship between the amount of property owned and the probability that a property holder would be an activist. Of the 85 investor-speculators in the top decile of property owners, 64.7% were activists; of the 435 homeowners in the bottom five deciles, however, only 39.0% were activists. This means that nearly half of the total 863 male householders who owned property were activists, and they controlled the large majority of the total real estate in Cincinnati in 1838.

This analysis indicates that the total group of 1,194 activists included some representatives from every demographic category and socioeconomic class of the Cincinnati community in 1840, but that householders from certain sectors of the community were more active in voluntary associations than others. This unequal representation of householders in associational activity can be illustrated by comparing the portion of activists and householders in the twelve different sectors of the conical model of the community. At one extreme, the upper-class old settlers represented 2.7% of the householders but 16.1% of the activists; at the other extreme, the lower-class new settlers represented 17.7% of the householders but only .5% of the activists. A comparison between the proportion of the activists and householders in each of these twelve sectors indicates that four of them—all of the upper-class householders and the upper-middle-class old settlers—were considerably overrepresented in associational activity; that three of them—the remaining upper-middle-class householders and the middle-class old settlers—were proportionally represented; and that five of them—the remaining middle-class householders and the lower-class householders—were considerably underrepresented.

This suggests that two-thirds of the upper-class and upper-middle-class old settlers were activists; a fifth of the remaining upper-middle-class householders and middle-class old settlers were activists; and less than a twentieth of the remaining middle-class and lower-class householders were activists. In terms of the conical model, over half of the

Table 4.4   Proportion of Activists and Householders in
Sectors of the Cone

Sector	% of Householders	% of Activists	Activist Index	% of Householders Who Were Activists
Upper-class old settlers	2.7	16.1	5.9	75.8
Upper-class recent settlers	1.7	8.9	5.2	65.5
Upper-class new settlers	.2	1.0	5.0	63.3
Upper-middle-class old settlers	4.7	24.5	5.2	66.9
Upper-middle-class recent settlers	6.5	14.8	2.3	29.9
Upper-middle-class new settlers	8.3	9.1	1.1	14.2
Middle-class old settlers	7.6	7.7	1.0	13.2
Middle-class recent settlers	15.2	6.1	.4	5.3
Middle-class new settlers	29.9	10.0	.3	4.3
Lower-class old settlers	1.1	.3	.3	3.8
Lower-class recent settlers	3.8	.5	.1	1.7
Lower-class new settlers	17.7	.5	.15	.3
Total	99.4	99.5	1.0	13.7

activists were located in the four top and central sectors, which constituted less than a tenth of the householders, while less than a fifth of the activists were located in the five lower sectors outside and below the core of the middle class, where two-thirds of the householders were located.

The conclusion that voluntary associations did not attract the large majority of Cincinnatians is supported by an examination of the available membership records of some of the more broadly based local organizations and major religious denominations. In every organization, the actual members represent a small minority of the potential members: for example, volunteer fire companies—which were the pride of the city and whose work affected every resident—numbered 1,284 men, or less than a sixth of the male householders in 1840; and the chamber of commerce—which played an important role in the economic development of the city—numbered 270 members, or an eighth of the men engaged in commercial activities in 1840. A similar pattern is evident in the membership statistics of the major religious denominations: only a minority of the number of residents who were reported to be affiliated with each denomination were actually recorded as communicants or members of churches. The six Presbyterian churches numbered 1,841 communicants, or less than a third of their reported 6,000 adherents. The four Methodist churches listed 2,260 members, or approximately 45% of their reported 5,000 adherents. The two Episcopal churches had 259 communicants, or less than an eighth of their reported 2,000 adherents.

Minimum, Moderate, and Maximum Activists

Of the total group of activists, the majority were participants in only one category of informal association, usually a political meeting, and had an index of associational activity of 1. These 603 minimum activists, who represented 50.5% of the total group of 1,194 activists, were responsible for less than a fourth of the associational activity in Cincinnati during this period.

Four hundred and seventy-four activists, or nearly 40% of the total group, had an index of associational activity of more than 1 and less than 5. Some of these moderate activists participated in several different categories of informal associations, others were officeholders in formal organizations, and a few were active in both informal and formal associations. These moderate activists accounted for nearly half of the associational activity in the city in the years 1839–42. Their number included well-known residents of Cincinnati.

Lyman Beecher, the head of the Lane Theological Seminary and prominent Presbyterian minister, participated in several benevolent meetings and was on the board of trustees of Lane, giving him an index of 3. Charles Cist was a participant in a Democratic meeting, and attended a benevolent group activity, and served as a trustee of the Medical College, giving him an index of 4. Nicholas Longworth had an index of 3, having participated in an abolition meeting, a meeting of the Ohio Mechanics Institute, and several meetings concerning banking reform. Timothy Walker, who complained in his diary that his law practice, a new wife, and his law school duties gave him little free time, attended a large Whig rally and served as the head of the law school of the Cincinnati College, giving him an index of 3.[15]

One hundred and seventeen activists had an index of associational activity of 5 or more and can be described as maximum activists. Al-

Table 4.5   Index of Associational Activity

	Index of Activity	No. of Activists	No. of Acts
Minimum	1	603 (50.5)	603 (23.2)
Moderate	2	259 (21.7)	518 (19.9)
	3	134 (11.2)	402 (15.5)
	4	81 (6.8)	324 (12.5)
Maximum	5	44 (3.7)	220 (8.5)
	6	27 (2.3)	162 (6.2)
	7	18 (1.5)	126 (4.8)
	8	19 (1.6)	152 (5.8)
	9	4 (.3)	36 (1.4)
	10	4 (.3)	40 (1.5)
	11	1 (.1)	11 (.4)
Total		1,194	2,594

Note: Numbers in parentheses are percentages.

though these 117 maximum activists represent less than a tenth of the total number of 1,194 activists and less than 2% of the total number of 8,684 men listed in the *Directory for 1840,* they were responsible for more than a quarter of the 2,594 associational acts in Cincinnati during the three-year period, 1839–42.

In social composition, these 117 maximum activists stand out as a remarkably homogeneous group, distinguished by their greater experience and success, within the relatively heterogeneous population of the larger community. Nearly two-thirds of these men were old settlers, most of whom were over forty years old, while less than a tenth were new settlers, none of whom were under thirty years of age. Only 2 of these maximum activists had been born in Germany; of the 106 native-born Americans, two-thirds came from northeastern states. The maximum activists included no laborers, only 1 clerk, and 18 mechanics; two-thirds of these 117 men were from the occupational upper class, including 35 merchants, 24 officials, and 15 professionals. Two-thirds of the maximum activists owned real estate in 1838, and the 32 investor-speculators represented over a third of the entire group of property holders in the top decile. In terms of the conical model, only 6 maximum activists were middle- or lower-class new settlers while 65 were upper- or upper-middle-class old settlers in the top central portion of the cone.

More significantly, these 117 maximum activists can be described as a *power elite* in the community. Adapting the criteria of contemporary community power studies to the historical sources, most of this group qualifies according to each of the three separate methods of elite identification. All of these men were participants in informal meetings that can be considered the local *decisional* area, and they were active in an average of nearly half of the different categories of informal associations. All but one of these maximum activists were officeholders, half in more than one formal organization, and can be considered to be part of the *positional* elite of the community. And 86 appeared prominently in the *Biographical Index* of the Cincinnati Historical Society (52 of them with some formal biography), which suggests that they also achieved some *reputational* distinction in the general history of the city.

The importance of a high level of associational activity in determining a leadership position in the community and the degree to which these 117 maximum activists represent a power elite in Cincinnati in 1840 can be illustrated by an examination of the internal operation of the Cincinnati Chamber of Commerce, an analysis of the composition of the most important honorary committees during this period, and a review of the careers of two of the leading maximum activists. In each case a broad range of involvement and influence in voluntary associations seems to have been a distinguishing criteria for leadership; and in each case the maximum activists represented at least a substantial portion of the total number of men designated, according to contemporary evidence, as the power elite of the community.

The minutes of the Cincinnati Chamber of Commerce illustrate the importance of a high level of associational activity as a distinguishing characteristic of men chosen to leadership positions. This organization of prominent Cincinnati businessmen was founded in October 1839 to regulate and promote local trade. Of the 76 founding members, 52 were activists; of the 9 original officers, 5 were maximum activists. During its first year of existence, the chamber of commerce met nearly every week, admitting new members, forming committees, and transacting business. According to the minutes, 127 members took part in some organizational activity during this twelve-month period. Of the total 338 individual actions reported in the minutes, however, 130 were accounted for by the 9 officers, 84 were accounted for by 7 members, each of whom was responsible for at least 5 individual actions, while the remaining 124 were spread out among 111 other members.[16]

At every weekly meeting a committee of arbitration was elected, and at the end of the year a new board of officers was chosen. An analysis of these elections indicates that the men who were elected and those who were rejected were very similar in their social characteristics, but the former group invariably had been more active in the organization than the latter. Of the new board of officers elected in December 1840, for example, six of the original officers, who were responsible for an average of fifteen individual actions each, were reelected; the three original officers who were not reelected were responsible for an average of only nine individual actions, however, and were replaced by three of the most active non-officers, who had been responsible for an average of fourteen individual actions each during the preceding twelve-month period. This pattern suggests that, particularly in organizations composed of men with very similar backgrounds and interests, the most active and experienced members were chosen to leadership positions.

The same pattern is evident in the composition of the honorary committees that presided over special community occasions. Unfortunately, there is no indication of when, by whom, or how these select committees were chosen, but it is significant that although many of the names changed in each case, the majority of the men on each committee were activists, and generally half of these men were maximum activists. The eighteen men on the executive committee of the Semi-Centennial Celebration, for example, were all activists, and ten of them—Robert Buchanan, A. H. Ernst, John P. Foote, Daniel Gano, Joseph Graham, William Greene, Edward D. Mansfield, N. C. Read, J. C. Vaughan, and J. J. Wright—were maximum activists. Together these eighteen men held offices in five different banks and insurance companies, eight educational and philanthropic organizations, two fraternal organizations, and three fire companies, and four of them were on city council. Most, if not all, of these men can be considered to be part of the power elite of the community and their wide range of involvement and influence in local affairs was probably instrumental in the success of the Semi-Centennial Celebration.[17]

Finally, the careers of two of the leading maximum activists during this period—Robert Buchanan and Elam P. Langdon—illustrate the importance of associational activity in defining their position in the community. Both men were extremely active in a wide range of voluntary associations and, according to their biographies and personal papers, this kind of activity was instrumental in their success and prestige in the city. Although they do not use the term, the evidence clearly indicates that they were part of the power elite of Cincinnati.

The man with the highest index of activity, 11, was Robert Buchanan. During the three-year period 1839–42, Buchanan was an officer of two formal organizations—president of both the Canal Insurance Company and the Western Academy of Natural Sciences—and a participant in seven different types of meetings. Buchanan participated in at least four different Whig meetings, serving as an officer of the Hamilton County Executive Committee; he attended the Benevolent Ball and was a manager of the Boatmen's Bethel; he was a sponsor of the Cincinnati Fuel Oil Company; he attended the meeting organized to purchase a painting of Amerigo Vespucci; he participated in three different meetings to improve commercial relations with the South; he served as a judge of the Ohio Mechanics Institute Exhibition and as a chairman of the Merchant's Meeting; and finally, he signed his name to a petition not to repeal the bankruptcy law, a petition in favor of Free Banking, and one in support of a committee to study the Free Banking Law.

Buchanan's career epitomizes that of many of the group of maximum activists. Born in Meadville, Pennsylvania, in 1797, he left home by canoe at the age of fourteen, "having all my worldly possessions tied in a pocket handkerchief." For five years he served as a merchant's apprentice in Pittsburgh, then engaged in business in West Union, Ohio, until 1821, and then he acted as captain of the steamboat Maysville, which plied between New Orleans and Cincinnati. In 1823 Buchanan went into the grocery business in Cincinnati, first with Charles Macalester and Company, later in his own firm. During the next half century, Buchanan wrote, he was "concerned in six commercial houses, three cotton factories, one steam engine factory, one rolling mill, three banks and five steamboats."

In his "Sketch of a Busy Life," Buchanan listed over forty offices, "some of them of trust, others of a commercial, social, and benevolent character," which were "given without the slightest solicitation on my part, and many others refused, especially those of a political nature." Buchanan corresponded with many prominent local and national leaders and the tone of the correspondence suggests that he generally assumed an air of authority in his own letters and was replied to, in most cases, with a measure of respect and deference.[18]

Elam P. Langdon, with an index of associational activity of 10, was a trustee of the Cincinnati Public Schools, vice president of the Society for the Promotion of Useful Knowledge, director of the Cincinnati Savings Institute and the Equitable Insurance Company, and treasurer of the Odd Fellows Lodge. Besides these offices in formal organizations, Langdon participated in four different Democratic party functions, served on a ward temperance committee, loaned a painting for a Fine Arts benefit, and attended a teachers' meeting. He was also a member of the Independent Fire Company and, later, a stockholder in the Cincinnati Astronomical Society.

Langdon was born in Massachusetts in 1794, the son of a prominent Methodist preacher. He came to Cincinnati in 1806, where he lived with the William Burke family for several years, and entered the post office as a clerk in 1820. Early in his career, Langdon became a strong supporter of education, helping to establish the Apprentice's Library in 1821, serving as a public schools trustee, and, in later years, as trustee of Woodward College. For thirty-six years he remained in the post office, most of the time as assistant postmaster. In 1841, with the election of Harrison as president, such important patronage positions were now controlled by the Whigs rather than the Democrats, and Langdon feared that he would lose his office as well. Langdon's stature in the community, and his influence and regard among prominent local Whigs, is evident in his attempt to hold his office, detailed in his correspondence, which eventually succeeded. A long-standing friendship with Harrison, the personal intervention of Judge Jacob Burnet, a recommendation from city council, and broad support from citizens of both parties are cited in several letters as contributing to his chances for reappointment. Despite his clear identification as a Democrat, Langdon apparently succeeded because of his general esteem in the community, his reputation for competence and fairness, and the support he had from a number of influential Whig leaders in the city.[19]

Multiple Officeholding: An Interlocking Directorate

The pattern of broad involvement and influence throughout the associational network that distinguished the maximum activists in 1840 created a loose "interlocking directorate" within the major organizations in Cincinnati, composed of men who were officers in more than one formal organization. Of the 396 Cincinnatians who held power in some formal organization between 1839 and 1842, 78 were officers of at least two different categories of formal organizations. Although these 78 multiple officeholders represent only a fifth of the total number of officeholders during this period, they held nearly 40% of the total number of offices in Cincinnati formal organizations.

Because they were involved and influential in several different areas of local activity, these multiple officeholders had a broader and more comprehensive view of the affairs of the city than most Cincinnatians. Because their loyalties and responsibilities were divided, multiple officeholders were in a unique position to coordinate their different organizations. Because they served as links between particular voluntary associations, they can be described as mediators within the associational network.

These patterns of multiple officeholding also had important implications for the organizations in which these men held power. In general, the more multiple officeholders in a particular organization, the more ties it would have into the larger associational network and, by implication, the better it could cooperate with other organizations and coordinate their interests. If these linkages were restricted to several particular organizations, this may reflect a strong mutual interest. If there were a number of linkages diffused throughout the associational network, however, this probably reflected a broader and more general interest in the development of the community. And if there were no linkages between two organizations, this would suggest that there was probably little communication or cooperation between these groups.

An analysis of the pattern of multiple-officeholding in selected formal organizations indicates that there were definite ties between certain organizations in the city, but that these ties varied in intensity and direction. These formal organizations included six banks, eighteen benevolent and educational organizations, three city councils (from 1839 to 1842), fifteen masonic and Odd Fellows lodges, and twelve fire companies. Together, these organizations had 270 officers, 212 of whom were officers of a single organization, 55 of whom were officers of two organizations, and 3 of whom were officers of 3 or more different organizations.

An analysis of the 121 offices held by the 58 multiple officeholders

Table 4.6   Officers of Selected Formal Organizations

General Category	No. of Organizations	No. of Officers
Banks	6	55
Benevolent-educational	18	69
City council		44
Fraternal	15	43
Fire companies	12	59
Total	51	270

suggests an important difference among these formal organizations. All five categories of formal organizations included officers who also held positions in other categories of formal organizations, but the proportion differed considerably. Approximately a quarter of the officers of banks, city council, benevolent, and fraternal organizations, but only a tenth of those of fire companies, were officers in some other category of formal organizations at the same time. Within each category, more striking differences occur. Within the economic category, for example, sixteen of the twenty-six officers of the Cincinnati Savings Institution, but only five of the fifteen officers of the Ohio Life Insurance and Trust Company, were multiple officeholders. Within the governmental category, fourteen of the twenty-one city councilmen, but only three of the eleven township trustees, were multiple officeholders. These differences in the proportion of multiple officeholders within each formal organization suggest differences in their effective ties within the larger network of associations in the city.

More interesting are the linkages, through multiple officeholding, between each category of formal organizations. The strongest ties were between the banks, benevolent organizations, and city council. The weakest ties were between fire companies, benevolent organizations, and banks. Here, too, the ties between the individual organizations are most significant. Twelve of the twenty officers of the Fire Department Insurance Company, but only one bank officer, were officers of the Cincinnati Fire Association. Together the fourteen trustees of the Common Schools (or public schools) held six offices in other educational organizations and four offices in economic organizations, but only two were officers of fraternal organizations and one was a fire company official.

Table 4.7   Multiple-Officeholding in Formal Organizations

	Banks	Benevolent-Educational	City Council	Fraternal	Fire Companies	Total
Banks	x	8	4	1	1	14
Benevolent-educational	8	x	5	3	0	16
City council	4	5	x	2	1	12
Fraternal	1	3	2	x	4	10
Fire companies	1	0	1	4	x	6
Total multiple-officeholders	14	14	16	12	10	6
Total officers	55	69	44	43	59	
Multiple/total officers	25.4%	23.2%	27.2%	23.2%	10.2%	

Despite these clear patterns of overlapping officeholding, however, the Fire Department Insurance Company was the only formal organization with a majority of officers drawn from any other single organization. An examination of the other offices held by the officers of each of the banks, insurance companies, fraternal organizations, and fire companies reveals a rather diffused pattern, suggesting that there were no obvious clusters of organizations, with many common members, within the larger network of formal organizations. That is, no bank seemed to control, through its officers, any insurance company or educational institution, and the officers of the individual fire companies did not appear to affiliate with a particular fraternal group. This diffused pattern of multiple officeholding suggests that there were no clearly identifiable separate or competing subelites within the associational network.

Several conclusions can be drawn from this analysis. First, it is significant that the fire company officers were relatively unrepresented in other formal organizations and that most of their existing ties were with the fraternal groups. Ironically, despite the public service purpose of the fire companies and their relatively broad social composition, the officers of these groups were relatively uninvolved in the rest of the associational network. This may have been due to a preoccupation with this vital activity, it may have reflected a lack of interest in other affairs, or it may have indicated an exclusive or isolated attitude among the group. The fact that fire company ties were largely with insurance companies and fraternal groups suggests a rather narrow preoccupation with fire control and fellowship.

At the other extreme, it is significant that there were relatively strong ties between the bank boards, city council, and the benevolent organizations. The overlap of membership in these three groups is dramatized in the case of two men who were officers in all three organizations. S. S. L'Hommedieu—publisher of the Cincinnati *Gazette* and a large landowner in the city—was a director of the Lafayette Bank, president of the Apprentice's Library, and councilman from the Seventh Ward. James McCandless—owner of a large rolling mill—was a director of the Commercial Bank, president of the Manufacturer's Insurance Company, a director of the Ohio Mechanics Institute, and councilman from the Third Ward. The strong ties between the banks, benevolent, and governmental organizations, exemplified by these two men, suggest a broad concern for the relationship among the economic interests, educational development, and political life of the community.

The different voluntary associations in Cincinnati in 1840 can be considered a loose associational network tied together by certain common interests and members. Although each group and organization had a particular purpose and membership, the fact that every voluntary association included some men who were active in other voluntary associations tended to link them, in different directions and in varying degrees, within the larger associational network. These linkages, epitomized by the extensive involvement and influence of the maximum activists, created a comprehensive channel of communication and cooperation in the organization and operation of local affairs. In a larger sense, this associational network, particularly the interlocking directorate of multiple officeholders, represented the institutional framework for the general development of the city.

Just as extensive associational activity tended to reflect and reinforce a more cosmopolitan attitude in individuals—a concern and commitment to a broad range of local affairs—so strong ties within the associational network tended to establish a more corporate approach among particular organizations to community development. The fact that the activists, particularly the maximum activists, were predominantly the older and better-established members of the community, with relatively similar backgrounds and interests, suggests that they represented a limited and exclusive leadership group. The fact that these men were often involved and influential in a variety of associational activities, however, suggests that they developed a fairly broad knowledge of and commitment to local development.

From this perspective, therefore, the associational network represented a limited (in membership) but comprehensive (in activities) institutional context for the organizational life of the community. In terms of the conic model, each member of the community who was a member of a voluntary association was linked by this particular interest and involvement. Within the conic model, therefore, there were hundreds of discrete networks, representing each of the different voluntary associations in the city. Moreover, the fact that many of these men, particularly the maximum activists, were affiliated with several different voluntary associations, created linkages between these separate networks, forming the more complex interwoven associational network. Because most of these activists, particularly the maximum activists, were located in the central and upper portion of the cone, the network was concentrated and densest in this area in and near the apex of the cone. Although this area included only a fraction of the total community, or the total adult white male population of the city, it represented the nexus of the organizational structure of the city.

Internal Divisions: The Whigs and Democrats

One week in 1840, the buildings of Cincinnati were covered with large posters proclaiming "a grand Washingtonian mass meeting at the court house next Saturday night." The announcement included a long list of the "names of almost all of the leading, demure, and sober citizens of the city," who were sponsors of the meeting, and, in bold letters, the name of the featured speaker, "the people's great democratic orator, J. Wykoff Piatt, Esq.!!!" That evening the old room of the court of common pleas was "thronged with masses of citizens—on the floor, in the bar, on the bench, and in the gallery, every place was filled with people." In time, "one of our chief citizens was called upon to preside, and vice-presidents and secretaries too numerous to mention, were duly nominated and appointed by the meeting, for in those days the meetings did these things themselves, and were not instructed or commanded by committees of any sort or kind whatsoever."[20]

Finally, Mr. Piatt was introduced and "he took his majestic stand before the assembled people." Born in Kentucky in 1801, Piatt came to Cincinnati as a young man and soon established himself as one of the leading members of the local bar. During the three-year period 1839–42, Piatt was a maximum activist who addressed a meeting to organize the Cincinnati Eye Infirmary, was on a review of the Ohio Mechanics Institute, was an officer of the Society for the Promotion of Useful Knowledge, was clerk of the court of common pleas, and chaired the executive committee of the Hamilton County Democratic Party. As the acknowledged leader of the Democratic Party of Hamilton County, Piatt, who had great influence with the Irish Democrats, was torn between his identification with his party's opposition to any attempt to control the sale or consumption of liquor and his sense of commitment and responsibility to the corporate interests of the local leadership group, which supported temperance efforts. After considerable coaxing and cajolery by numerous influential local leaders, Piatt finally agreed to speak to the people on the subject of temperance.[21]

"With a great snort and a great blow and a fume, and with a very high pitched tone of voice, Piatt commenced his 'F-e-l-l-o-w C-i-t-i-z-e-n-s!' " He told the audience that, for himself, he had always been a temperance man, and that nobody had ever seen him drunk. He then proceeded into a long review of the history of the temperance movement, which "consumed about three-quarters of an hour in talk, but not one iota of applause did he get from the crowd." Piatt became confused, being accustomed to enthusiastic, vociferous support from his audiences, and proceeded slowly, in a hesitant, bumbling fashion. Just as he was citing a scriptural statement on the question of drinking, "to use a little wine for the stomach's sake," a "big, burly, boisterous butcher boy" came into the hall, and assuming that Piatt was in agreement with the statement of Saint Paul, shouted: *"Go it, Piatt: Give these temperance fellars h-ll!"* With this, the audience erupted with shouts and hurrahs, and Piatt suddenly changed course, saying: "ah, yes, my fellow citizens—my fellow d-e-m-o-c-r-a-t-s—and the good Saint Paul was *right*—right—all right." And Piatt turned on the leaders of the meeting, who immediately exited, and finished with a rousing denunciation of any efforts to limit the free sale and consumption of alcohol in the city.[22]

This story is interesting in part because it illustrates the manner in which popular meetings were organized and conducted during this period; more important, it indicates a fundamental division within the community between the Whigs and Democrats that is evident in an analysis of election returns, the social composition of the political activists, and the political affiliation of the maximum activists. This analysis indicates that, in 1840, the difference between the Whigs and Democrats can be described not only in terms of social composition—the Whigs were typically the older, better established, and more successful householders located in the central and upper portion of the cone while the Democrats were predominantly younger, less settled, middle- and lower-class householders located in the outer and lower portions of the cone—but also, and perhaps more suggestively, in terms of their relative degree of involvement and influence in the associational network. The Whigs were considerably more active in voluntary associations than the Democrats and included the large majority of the maximum activists. These structural differences between the two parties can also be related to some of the differences in their political philosophies and help to explain the political changes that occurred in Cincinnati after 1840.

In the 1840 presidential election, which drew more Cincinnatians to the polls than any previous election, there were 6,340 votes cast in the community. Although there was great interest in the election, which offered residents their first chance to put a fellow-Cincinnatian in the White House, and a prominent local editor reported that "nearly the entire vote of the city was polled," this figure represented only half of the total adult white male population of the city, and only 73% of the total 8,684 householders listed in the *Directory for 1840.*

During the three-year period 1839–42, 749 householders were listed in newspaper accounts that identified their political affiliation. In many cases their names appeared on long lists of the names of people supporting the party, which appeared in the local press just before election day. Some were officers or participants at meetings, or had offered their services as members of party "vigilance committees" for election day. These 749 Cincinnatians whose political affiliation is known—448 Whigs and 301 Democrats—represented 11.8% of the 6,340 citizens who voted in the 1840 election. Although certainly not a representative sample of the total Cincinnati electorate, these 749 Cincinnatians included many rank-and-file political activists.

The first, and most important thing to notice is that, of the total number of names included in the Whig and Democratic newspaper lists, 76% of the Whigs appeared in Shaffer's *Directory for 1840,* but only 55% of the Democratic names were householders. The Whigs, therefore, included almost a third more members of the community than the Democrats; or, from the opposite perspective, the Democrats had almost twice as many political activists not included in the community as the Whigs. The fact that only slightly more than half of the Democrats were listed in the *Directory for 1840* probably reflects the high number of active Democrats from outlying townships, where Democratic strength was concentrated. It also suggests that the Democrats were less well established in the community than the Whigs. The fact that better than three-fourths of the Whigs were listed in the *Directory for 1840* indicates, conversely, that Whig strength was concentrated within the city and that the party included many of the better-established citizens of the total population.

An analysis of the social composition of these political activists indicates clear differences between the Whigs and Democrats. With regard

Table 4.8   Social Composition of Political Activists

	N	% Whig	% Democrat
Priority			
Old Settler	277	68	32
New Settler	155	41	59
Nativity			
Yankee	105	76	24
Buckeye	462	59	41
Great Britain	100	53	47
German States	46	41	59
Occupation			
Upper-class	275	69	31
Middle-class	356	53	47
Lower-class	65	42	58
Wealth			
Property holder	287	72	28
Level			
Minimum activist	492	50	50
Moderate activist	166	72	28
Maximum activist	91	82	18
Participation			
Philanthropic	123	80	20
Mutual aid	44	77	23
Slavery	43	63	37
Patron	45	84	16
Friend	22	77	23
Professional	16	76	24
Bank issue	68	78	22
Power			
Economic	69	83	17
Benevolent	31	74	26
Governmental	94	74	26
Fraternal	23	69	31
Fire company	25	69	31
Total	749	59	41

to priority, a majority of the new settlers were Democrats while the old settlers were predominantly Whigs; this suggests that relative length of residence, stability, and maturity were of some influence in determining political affiliation. With regard to nativity, most of the Yankees were Whigs, and to a lesser degree, so were the men born in England, New York, New Jersey, and Pennsylvania; however, a larger proportion of the men born in the southern and border states and a majority of the immigrants from Ireland and Germany were Democrats. With regard to occupation, most of the men in the occupational upper class were Whigs while the men in the occupational middle and lower classes were more likely to be Democrats. In wealth, the large majority of the property holders were Whigs, and the proportion of Whigs was greatest in the higher deciles.

Second, when we turn to the index of associational activity of these political activists, it is clear that the Whigs were considerably more active in voluntary associations than the Democrats. Three out of four of the Democrats, but only half of the Whigs, were minimal activists who were involved in no other category of associational activity than politics. At the other extreme, of the 91 maximum activists who were political participants, 75 were Whigs and only 16 were Democrats. Of the 325 political participants who were involved in some category of associational activity beside political associations, the 87 Democrats were responsible for 299 acts (average index of associational activity: 3.4) while the 238 Whigs were responsible for 951 acts (average index of associational activity: 4.1). This means that, of the total 1,849 nonpolitical acts within the associational network, over half were by Whigs while less than a sixth were by Democrats.

Despite this clear dominance by the Whigs throughout the associational network, there were some interesting differences in the patterns of participation and power by the activists of these two parties. At one extreme, over three-quarters of the patrons of the arts, Friends of the South, and officers of economic organizations were Whigs; at the other extreme, over a third of the men involved in the slavery issue (33% of the abolitionists, and 40% of the anti-abolitionists), and nearly a third of the officers of fire companies and fraternal organizations were Democrats. Democrats represented a majority of the political activists of only two meetings (one to form a workingmen's party, the other for state banking reform) and two formal organizations (a fire company and an Odd Fellows lodge). The fact that nearly every voluntary association included members of both political parties suggests that, although Whigs were considerably more active than Democrats throughout the associational network, voluntary associations were not exclusively identified with a particular party.

Clearly, the index of associational activity measures something very different from priority, nativity, wealth, or occupation and must be treated differently. But it is significant that of these five different variables, this index appears to have the highest correlation with political affiliation:

	χ *Square*	*Cramer's V*
Index of associational activity	57.69 (9df)	.2773
Property value	51.45 (9df)	.2622
Nativity	45.14 (9df)	.2456
Priority	32.19 (9df)	.2074
Occupation	29.12 (9df)	.1973

This is significant not only because the index suggests an important difference between the two parties but also because it suggests a new complementary dimension to the understanding of political parties.

The very different patterns of involvement in voluntary associations by the Whigs and Democrats can be related to their respective political ideologies. To oversimplify considerably, it is significant that the Whigs, who were generally active in voluntary associations, often in many different areas of activity, had a more organic, corporate attitude toward society and stressed the importance of cooperation (often through voluntary associations) in achieving social progress; while the Democrats, who were less active in voluntary associations, particularly a wide range of different associations within the associational network, had a more individualistic, atomized view of society and argued for a more laissez-faire social environment in which individuals would compete against one another.

The Fragmentation of the Old Order

Voluntary associations and political parties both play an important role in the functional organization and operation of communities, particularly during periods of rapid development. The Jacksonian period was in many respects dominated and defined by these two distinctively American institutions, and their influence was most evident in the cities. Each of these institutions was a means by which the individual could transcend the limited world of family, friends, and neighborhood and work to become an active part of the larger society. Each of these institutions represented a particular context for citizens to join together, to improve themselves and their community. In very different ways, each was an important instrument for leadership and social change.

During the years before the Civil War, voluntary associations and politics both played an important part in the development of Cincinnati. However, the emphasis of these two institutions was very different. Voluntary associations generally had a clearly defined purpose, an identifiable and limited membership, and were not usually in direct competition with one another. Political parties, on the other hand, despite their well-articulated ideological differences, were more concerned with attaining office than with achieving their principles; they included much broader and more heterogeneous constituencies, and consequently, they were in constant competition. Because of these basic differences in organization and purpose, voluntary associations and political parties had very different effects on communities. Because voluntary associations usually were not competing with one another, in purpose or for members, they were more compatible and engendered a more corporate concept of society. Because political parties were in direct conflict with one another, over principles and popular support, they were more divisive and encouraged a more fragmented concept of society.

At midcentury, the roles and relative influence of these two institutions gradually changed in Cincinnati, reflecting and reinforcing a fundamental transformation in the general organization of the community. During the late 1840s and early 1850s, the role of voluntary associations became increasingly restricted and specialized while political parties became more comprehensive in their appeal and influence. As a result of these organizational changes, politics gradually replaced voluntary associations as the main institution for social change. However, because of the very different orientations of politics and voluntary associations, the effect of this transition was increasing internal conflict within the community and the fragmentation of the old corporate order. This transition was dramatically demonstrated in 1851 in the Fire Company Riots, and in the Democratic capture of the city the preceding year.

Volunteer fire companies were the oldest, largest, and most effective local organizations in the early history of Cincinnati, and at least through 1840, they were proudly cited as examples of community cooperation and civic spirit. Although most Cincinnatians were not actually members of fire companies at this time, they were the most broad-based voluntary association in the community, and they included, at least as honorary members, many of the older, established leadership group. Despite their social orientation, and a strong competitive spirit, the fire companies generally worked together in fighting fires. But during the late 1840s and early 1850s, the character and composition of many of the fire companies changed: "The older members of the fire companies by the lapse of years and for other reasons had passed out of service and in their places were many younger or less public spirited men who regarded a fire simply as an occasion for starting a riot. The engine houses had become loafing places for the members and their friends and the firemen a gang of political parasites controlled by the lower class of politicians."[23]

During the late 1840s fire companies began to engage in "washing out" operations on particular "houses of ill repute." By 1850 local newspapers regularly carried reports of various threats and fights between individual fire companies, and the number of local fires, many suspected to have been caused by arson, skyrocketed. In the fall of 1851, when the Western Hose Company, No. 3, and the Washington Company, No. 1, clashed en route to a fire at a planing mill, other companies joined in the fracas, which turned into an all-night riot. The inability of Mayor Mark P. Taylor, a former president of the Cincinnati Fire Association, to stop this riot, the eruption of other similar attacks, and escalating insurance rates angered many Cincinnatians, but the volunteer fire companies were an entrenched local institution supported by former members and many of the new political leaders. A campaign to replace the volunteer fire companies with a paid professional fire department—led by Timothy Walker, Miles Greenwood, and J. W. Piatt—was, at first, very unpopular, and the members of city council, who privately admitted the need for reform, were afraid to vote publicly for it. Only when a new steam fire engine, built and operated by the reformers, outperformed an old hand-operated engine, did public opinion change and accept a new municipal fire department. The success of this reform movement was widely heralded as a triumph of modern technology and professionalism, but the demise of the volunteer fire companies also marked an unfortunate decline in cooperation and civic spirit, which was gradually replaced by a partisan political spirit of competition and conflict.

The Fire Company Riots were one manifestation of the rise of political interest and partisanship in Cincinnati. During the 1830s and early 1840s the Whigs had dominated local politics: in state and national elections, the Whigs polled around 60% of the Cincinnati vote and generally carried all of the city's wards; in local elections, which were not explicitly defined along national party lines, the Whigs maintained the majority of seats on city council and successfully promoted their program of internal improvements. During the late 1840s, however, this Whig hegemony was challenged by Democrats, who, with the help of the large German vote, captured political control of the city in 1850. In the 1848 presidential election, for the first time since 1828, the Democratic candidate, Zachary Taylor, carried the city, with 52.2% of the local vote. Two years later, in the 1850 election for city council, the Democratic candidates captured twenty-one out of the thirty-six seats, thanks to "a larger vote by several thousand than ever before."

The Democrats' triumph in Cincinnati was the result of a number of particular local and national conditions—the increasing German vote, new ward lines, nativism, stronger party organization, and the gradual realignment of political parties—but it reflected a general reorientation within the community. The old and relatively cohesive associational network that had tied the minority of activists together into a functional unit was increasingly split, around midcentury, and gradually replaced by the new and more inclusive divisions of partisan politics. As the proportion of the population voting increased, from 8.8% in 1820, to 13.4% in 1840, to 16.5% in 1860, the proportion of the population holding office in formal organizations decreased, from 1.2% in 1820, to .9% in 1840, to .4% in 1860, and the mean number of offices these men held dropped from 1.9 in 1820, to 1.5 in 1840, to 1.2 in 1860. The increasing fragmentation of the Cincinnati community that resulted from this gradual reorientation was evident in 1852, when Louis Kossuth, the Hungarian revolutionary hero, visited Cincinnati. "The society of Cincinnati lacks cohesion," his traveling companion, Francis Pulsky, noted; a general parade was canceled due to conflicts over who was to ride in the carriage with the distinguished guest and Kossuth finally had to make separate appearances before " 'the big people' of Cincinnati at a banquet, and others again at Nixon's hall, and then the ladies and Northern Germans, and the Southern Germans, and the fashionable public at large, and the lower classes at large." This fragmentation of the community was also evident in an editorial in the Cincinnati *Enquirer* in 1850 describing the recent celebration of the Fourth of July: "We had no regular old fashioned way of celebrating the day as it used to be done fifteen or twenty years ago—by a regular turnout of the citizens, a procession, an oration delivered, winding up with a dinner, at which innumerable toasts were drunk. That is a fashion which seems to have become obsolete. The way the day is celebrated of late years is truly an *independent* style: the whole community did not join together in it."[24]

Afterword

John D. Fairfield

Walter Stix Glazer's study of antebellum Cincinnati teaches us about both urbanization in mid-nineteenth-century America and the discipline of urban history at the end of the 1960s. Readers should be aware of the absence of detailed accounts of the role of women, labor, and African Americans in the city's life, an absence that underscores the advances historians have made on these fronts and that can be rectified through supplementary reading.[1] But what is most remarkable about *Cincinnati in 1840* is how much it illuminates past and present historical debates.

Writing in the 1960s amid an explosion of interest in the history of American cities, Glazer helped to create the "new urban history." Spurred by Arthur Schlesinger's *The Rise of the City* and Richard Wade's *The Urban Frontier,* the new urban historians hoped to place the city at the center of American history. As Wade had, they challenged Frederick Jackson Turner's "frontier thesis." Examining "the significance of the frontier in American history," Turner had argued that the experience of winning a succession of frontiers explained American development. In laying the foundation for an interpretation of "the significance of the city in American history," Glazer joined the search for an "urban thesis" that would put urbanization at the center of American historical development.[2]

Glazer's use of quantitative methods reflected the new urban historians' effort to craft a "history from the bottom up," just as his use of social scientific theories reflected their desire to develop an interdisciplinary approach to the city. Yet Glazer still understood that the things people actually thought, said, and did remain the essential stuff of history. As a storyteller, Glazer used what was sometimes derisively called "anecdotal" evidence to convey ideological pressures in the city. No statistic, no sociological theory could capture the meaning of the "deep melancholia" and eventual suicide of Cincinnati's Minister to the Poor (Chap. 3). The powerful narrative of *Cincinnati in 1840* has continued to attract readers when much of the new urban history has been forgotten.

As a new urban historian, Glazer engaged new ambitions and methods. But in investigating the character of American democracy, he joined the oldest debate in American historiography. Where Alexis de Tocqueville had found egalitarianism, mediocrity and anarchic self-reliance in Jacksonian America, Glazer located a functioning and complex social system, initially directed by an elite minority but evolving toward pluralism. Revising Tocqueville with the use of the concepts of "power elites," "interlocking directorates," and "pluralism," Glazer contributed to a Cold War debate about the openness and efficacy of American democracy.[3]

But *Cincinnati in 1840* is more than a window on past historical debates. Doubts about "the validity and future of democracy," Glazer wrote in the original manuscript, had never been higher than in the wake of the election of Andrew Jackson. Changing "democracy" to "the republic" (which, in fact, the copy editor has done) invites comparison to the current argument about the impact of civic republicanism and liberal capitalism on American democracy. Ever since the conversations between Tocqueville and his Queen City acquaintances with which Glazer's study begins, the Jacksonian city has been recognized as a key site in the clash between America's civic and economic ambitions. Antebellum urbanization generated difficult choices between a revolutionary, republican ideal of virtuous, independent citizens pursuing the commonwealth and the acquisitive liberal capitalist (Tocquevillean) ethic that drove the market revolution. The problem for historians has been to explain how and to what extent social and economic tensions arising from a market and capitalist transformation were or were not translated into political conflicts.[4]

When Glazer wrote, modernization theory had emerged as the latest explanation of the relationship between socioeconomic change and political behavior. In Glazer's words, modernization theory held that each "community has a distinctive ideology, demography, social structure, and leadership, but these differences can be related, roughly, to particular stages of structural evolution" (from the Introduction). Modernization theory, in other words, posited that ideas and culture developed more or less in lockstep with underlying and determining structural forces. Glazer proposed to supplant the ill-defined transition from "community" to "society" (of which modernization theory was only the most recent version) with a fuller account of urban development. As a result, *Cincinnati in 1840* put a changing civic culture, rather than impersonal historical forces or structural imperatives, at the center of Cincinnati's transition from "community" to "society."[5]

A community ideology, Glazer argued, gave early Cincinnatians a common identity and purpose that unified the city and promoted its growth, even as it exaggerated the harmony of interests. By the 1840s, class, ethnic, and racial divisions had strained the social order and led to a disintegration of what we would call the civic culture of republicanism. A self-constituted moral elite retreated into its own exclusive social spaces and institutions. Still politically powerful, this elite was less open to the participation of the lower classes, who were increasingly defined as the major problem facing the city. Social stratification and the erosion of civic cooperation coincided with and were partially responsible for the city's economic stagnation relative to other midwestern cities.[6]

Glazer concludes that a shift in political practice, as much as social and economic structures, transformed Cincinnati's civic culture. Glazer found that the voluntary associations Tocqueville so admired for diluting American individualism had indeed encouraged cooperation and reinforced "a more corporate concept of society." Volunteer fire companies, for example, cooperated effectively to put out fires. The subsequent rise of political parties, supplanting voluntary associations in political life and struggling against one another, forged a more competitive view of society. Once taken over by a partisan spirit and party membership, the fire companies showed more interest in brawling and rioting than in putting out fires. The shift to a professionalized fire department, Glazer concluded, was widely embraced but "also marked an unfortunate decline in cooperation and civic spirit." A system of professional and partisan politics had introduced more selfish, particularistic interests and made them the central focus of civic life. It may also have contributed to the "disengagement" and "engaged disbelief" modern historians have found among citizens of the Jacksonian city. Glazer rediscovered what the revolutionary generation had understood: political practice shaped the mind and character of the citizen. Civic virtue was the product, not the precondition, of a good political system.[7]

Notes

Introduction

1. George W. Pierson, *Tocqueville and Beaumont in America* (New York, 1938), 52.
2. Ibid., 555, 557, 561, 565.
3. Ibid., 557.
4. This information is implicit in much of the history written since the 1830s, when the first generation of nationalist historians, particularly George Bancroft, extolled the triumph of democracy in America. It is argued, explicitly, in two essays: David Donald, "Toward a Reconsideration of the Abolitionists," in *Lincoln Reconsidered* (New York, 1955), and Rowland Berthoff, "The American Social Order: A Conservative Hypothesis," *American Historical Review* 65 (1960): 495–515.
5. Jewett to Willard, May 8, 1832, in the Jewett Papers, quoted from Daniel Aaron, "Cincinnati, 1818–1838: A Study of Attitudes in the Urban West" (Ph.D. diss., Harvard University, 1942). Aaron seems to have been the first person to appreciate the career and writings of Timothy Walker, and much of the following description follows his account. There is a good short biography of Walker in the *Dictionary of American Biography* and a longer account, including excerpts from some of his writings, in Clara Longworth de Chambrun, *The Making of Nicholas Longworth* (New York, 1933), 55–73.
6. There is no evidence that Tocqueville ever saw Walker's article. Pierson mentions Tocqueville's interview with Walker, and his high opinion of the young lawyer, but does not mention the *New England Magazine* article. Aaron, who quotes the article extensively and has identified it as Walker's, never explicitly draws the connection between the analyses of these two men, particularly the close correspondence between their concepts of individualism. Walker's reaction to *Democracy in America* was that it was "often able and ingenious but abounding in errors. What is extraordinary

is that he should understand America so well." Chambrun, *The Making of Nicholas Longworth,* 61.

7. *New England Magazine* 1 (1831): 30–35. The article was signed "W," but Aaron says he has conclusive evidence that the author was in fact Timothy Walker. This is supported by the similarity in style and phraseology between this article and other contemporary Walker articles.

8. Timothy Walker, *Annual Discourse Delivered at the Ohio Historical and Philosophical Society at Columbus on the 23rd of December, 1837* (Cincinnati, 1838), 16. Walker's own term for the excesses of democracy was "agrarianism," but he saw little chance that it would arise here.

9. This type of intensive, quantitative microscopic analysis of a single community within a limited period of time has been applied to the study of English society, particularly during the sixteenth and seventeenth centuries, and, more recently, for the colonial period in New England. The only such study of the nineteenth century, however, is the admirable analysis of Trempealeau County, Wis., testing the Turner Thesis, by Merle Curti, *The Making of an American Community* (Palo Alto, 1959).

10. In 1840 there were 44,142 white and 2,258 black residents in Cincinnati. All of the evidence, both impressionistic and quantitative, points to the fact that there was a separate white and black community, and that the two overlapped to only a slight extent. The census data includes African Americans, and David Shaffer's *Directory for 1840* includes a separate section of African Americans, but Cincinnati's African Americans were virtually excluded from the social structure, the associations, and the opportunities for mobility on which this study focuses. African Americans, therefore, are completely omitted from discussion in this community profile.

11. The terms *participation* and *power* are used in the special sense defined above, which corresponds only imperfectly with the common sense of the words. The distinction is based on the character of the source—newspaper versus guidebook or directory—but this incorporates the distinction between ephemeral informal groups and permanent formal organizations. Thus a man participates in an informal group—whatever his role or its function—but he has power if he is an officer in a formal organization. The implication, which is intentional, is that there is greater opportunity for democratic participation in informal than formal associations and that there is greater potential for power by an elite through a formal than an informal association.

12. In a very crude sense, participation and power correspond to the decisional and positional indexes used by social scientists to analyze community power structure. The historical record provides less precise evidence than

contemporary survey research methods, however, in determining the relevance and relative importance of meetings in terms of their decisions or offices in terms of their position. Because of the great variation within the informal groups in terms of their decisional importance, and within the formal offices in terms of their positional importance, no comprehensive analysis that corresponds to the contemporary studies can be made. The purpose of this analysis is only to measure the relative extent of activity across the associational network.

13. This measure of the reputation of the activists corresponds, in a rough sense, with the reputational index of social scientists because it reflects a general evaluation as by recognized authorities of their stature in the community. A list of men prominent in Cincinnati from 1818 to 1838 compiled by Aaron is also used here to determine whether the 1840 activists were prominent during the earlier period.

14. Stephen Thernstrom, one of the leading practitioners and proponents of the new urban history, has argued, persuasively, that it "lies squarely within the domain of social history, and for the student of modern society it is indeed nearly coterminous with social history." "The New Urban History," *Daedalus* (Spring 1971): 362.

15. Diamond quoted in Richard Wade, "An Agenda for Urban History" in Herbert J. Bass, ed., *The State of American History* (Chicago, 1970), 43–70.

16. A good historiographical review can be found in Charles N. Glaab, "The Historian and the American City: A Bibliographic Survey," in Phillip M. Hauser and Leo Schnore, eds., *The Study of Urbanization* (New York, 1865), 53–80.

  Eric F. Lampard, "American Historians and the Study of Urbanization," *American Historical Review* 67 (October 1961): 49–61; "The Dimensions of Urban History: A Footnote to the Urban Crisis," *Pacific Historical Review* 39 (August 1970): 261–78.

17. Louis Wirth, "Urbanism as a Way of Life," *American Journal of Sociology* 44 (July 1938): 1–24; Albert J. Reiss, Jr., "Urbanism," in Julius Gould and William L. Kolb, eds., *A Dictionary of the Social Sciences* (New York, 1955), 738–39.

18. This definition of community is derived from that of Roland Warren in *The Community of America* (Chicago, 1963), 21–53; Charles P. Loomis, *Social Systems: Essays on their Persistence and Change* (Princeton, 1960), 4.

19. Harold Kaufman, "Toward an Interactional Conception of Community," *Social Forces* 38 (October 1959): 8–17.

20. David L. Sills, "Voluntary Associations: Sociological Aspects," in Sills, ed., *International Encyclopedia of the Social Sciences* (New York, 1968), 16:362–79.

21. Robert Presthus, *Men at the Top: A Study in Community Power* (New York, 1964), 94–97.

22. Claire W. Gilbert, "Community Power and Decisionmaking; A Quantitative Examination of Previous Research," and Terry N. Clark, "Community Structure and Decision-Making," appear in Clark, ed., *Community Structure and Decision-Making: Comparative Analyses* (San Francisco, 1968).

23. Robert Dahl, *Who Governs: Democracy and Power in an American City* (New Haven, 1961); Stephen Thernstrom, *Poverty and Progress: Social Mobility in a Nineteenth Century City* (Cambridge, 1964), 225–41; Peter Rossi describes the study, but does not include the historical data ("The Organizational Structure of an American City," in Amitai Etzioni, *Complex Organizations: A Sociological Reader* [New York, 1961], 301–11). For Rossi's argument in "Power and Community Structure," see Clark, *Community Structure and Decision-Making,* 138. Robert O. Schulze, "The Bifurcation of Power in Satellite City," in Morris Janowitz, ed., *Community Political Systems* (New York, 1961), 19–80.

24. Sigmund Diamond, "From Organization to Society: Virginia in the Seventeenth Century," *American Journal of Sociology* 63 (March 1958): 457–75, is a brilliant example of this kind of analysis. Sam Bass Warner's *The Private City: Philadelphia in Three Periods of Its Growth* (Philadelphia, 1968), is a more ambitious, but less successful, study of this kind. Several non-American studies—Kenneth Little, *Western African Urbanization: A Study of Voluntary Associations in Social Change* (Cambridge, 1965), and Robert T. and Barbara G. Anderson, *The Vanishing Village: A Danish Maritime Community* (Seattle, 1964)—have stressed the importance of voluntary associations during the critical stage of rapid urbanization. This would suggest that the special demographic conditions—a high proportion of newcomers, without established family, friendship, or neighborhood contacts; developmental conditions; great demands for the coordination of many new activities—would, together, result in a relatively greater proportion of voluntary associations with a relatively more important role during this dynamic transitional stage.

25. John Higham has suggested that "the history of town and city is being transformed into the history of the community conceived of as a functioning whole." This provides the broad framework necessary to connect the many colonial communities studies and the urban biographies of the nineteenth and twentieth centuries. John Higham, *Writing American History: Essays on Modern Scholarship* (Bloomington, 1970), 163. Sam Hays, "The Evolution of the Social and Political Structure of the Modern American City" (typescript), is a cogent interpretation of the distinctive characteristics of cities in three stages of national history.

Chapter 1

1. Cincinnati *Chronicle,* December 29, 1838; *Whig,* December 27, 1838;
    January 2, 1839; *Daily Evening Post,* December 24, 26, 28, 1838; *Cincinnati Republican,* December 28, 1838; *Liberty Hall and Cincinnati Gazette,*
    January 10, 1839; Charles Theodore Greve, *Centennial History of Cincinnati and Representative Citizens* (Chicago, 1904), 605–6.
2. Discussions of these questions appear throughout the Cincinnati newspapers and various city directories and guidebooks and in many of the
    private collections of local citizens. Many of the travel accounts of visitors
    to the city during this period include these arguments as well. The pervasiveness of this local propaganda is suggested by one editor who, in a
    moment of critical detachment, noted that it became "dull to the westerner by repetition and vexatious to the easterner by contrast." *Hesperian* 3
    (1939): 497. A more positive assessment of the situation, however, suggested that this "vainglorious boasting" was, in fact, "prophetic and
    true." C. P. James, *Address Delivered Before the Citizen Guard* (Cincinnati,
    1842), 5.
3. This argument is presented in numerous newspaper articles and travel
    accounts but, most important, in the guidebooks of the period. The paradigm of this kind of literature—a model in its pervasive enthusiasm,
    extensive documentation, and general accuracy—is Charles Cist, *Cincinnati in 1841: Its Early Annals and Future Prospects* (Cincinnati, 1841).
4. James Hall, *Statistics of the West: At the Close of the Year 1836* (Cincinnati,
    1837), 217.
5. James Handasyd Perkins, *Memoir and Writings of James Handasyd Perkins,*
    edited by William H. Channing (Cincinnati, 1851), 2:367; Cincinnati
    Commercial and Literary Gazette, August 31, 1833.
6. Perkins, *Memoir and Writings,* 2:402; Cist, *Cincinnati in 1841,* 289.
7. Cist, *Cincinnati in 1841,* 82.
8. For a detailed description of the founding of Cincinnati, and the relationship between the three "original" settlements, Columbia, Losantiville,
    and North Bend, see Greve, *Centennial History of Cincinnati,* 142–316;
    Cist, *Cincinnati in 1841,* 14–29; and Francis W. Miller, *Cincinnati Beginnings; Missing Chapters in the Early History of the City and Miami Purchase*
    (Cincinnati, 1880).
9. See, for example, Charles Fenno Hoffman, *A Winter in the West* (New York,
    1835), 129; James Stuart, *Three Years in North America* (Edinburgh, 1833),
    474–75; Charles Augustus Murray, *Travels in North America during the
    Years 1834, 1835, and 1836* (London, 1839), 202–4; Godfrey T. Vigne, *Six
    Months in America* (Philadelphia, 1833), 133–34; James Edward Alex-

ander, *Transatlantic Sketches Comprising Visits to the Most Interesting Scenes in North and South America* (London, 1833), 2:123–24; Harriet Martineau, *Retrospect of Western Travel* (London, 1838), 2:215–69; Thomas Hamilton, *Men and Manners in America* (Edinburgh, 1833), 2:168–73; "Journal of Cyrus P. Bradley," *Ohio Archaeological and Historical Quarterly* 15 (1906):217–20; Charles Dickens, *American Notes* (New York, 1842), 195–96; James S. Buckingham, *The Eastern and Western States of America* (London, 1842), 2:381–86; Patrick Shirreff, *A Tour through North America* (Edinburgh, 1835), 281. The large number of favorable accounts of the city's appearance by nearly every visitor during this period suggests that Mrs. Trollope's infamous acidulous account reflects more her peculiar character than the actual condition of the city. Francis Trollope, *Domestic Manners of the Americans,* edited by Donald Smalley (New York, 1949), 39–42.

10. Cincinnati's population density, measured in terms of population per square mile of corporate area, was 14,480.6. Of the cities for which information is available, only Philadelphia (40,723.9), Pittsburgh (30,164.3), Saint Louis (23,527.1), and Boston (19,868) were denser; Baltimore (7,750.9), New Orleans (691.4), Washington (2,336.4), Buffalo (4,047.3), and Chicago (456.1) were considerably less dense. These data suggest that high population density was a characteristic of Cincinnati and some other cities during the pre–Civil War period. This argument is developed in a paper by Kenneth T. Jackson, "The Suburban Trend before the Civil War" (presented at the annual meeting of the American Historical Association, December 30, 1969). Data on the area of selected cities are drawn from R. D. McKenzie, *Metropolitan Community* (New York, 1933), 336–37.

11. For a vivid yet apparently accurate description of the slaughterhouses and their streamlined mass production operations, see Hoffman, *Winter in the West,* 133–34; Cist, *Cincinnati in 1841,* 238.

12. Charles Dickens, *American Notes,* 195–98; for Dickens's private comments on the city, which in this case were no less laudatory than his published account, see Charles Sumner Van Tassel, *Charles Dickens' 1842 Visit to Ohio* (n.p., 1937). Of the 6,781 buildings in Cincinnati in 1840, 3,315 had been built during the 1830s. This rose-colored description of Cincinnati's appearance was repeated by the numerous travelers' accounts cited above and portrayed in the several paintings and lithographs of the city done during this period. See especially the four street scene paintings of Cincinnati done by J. C. Wild in the 1830s and owned today by the Cincinnati Historical Society; the undersigned print of the waterfront in Robinson and Jones, *Cincinnati Directory for 1846* (Cincinnati, 1846). The Klauprecht and Menzel print in David Henry Shaffer, *Cincinnati Directory for*

1840 (Cincinnati, 1839), presents a slightly cruder picture which is probably more accurate considering the actual appearance in 1848 captured in the remarkable Fontayne and Porter daguerreotypes: see Carl Vitz, "The Cincinnati Waterfront—1848," *Bulletin of the Historical and Philosophical Society of Ohio* 6 (April 1948): 28–40.

13. For a series of discussions of economic conditions in Cincinnati that describes the impact and character of the depression, see the *Cincinnati Commercial*, February 28, April 16, 1840; January 6 and 20, March 4 and 11, 1841; *Cincinnati Republican*, April 8, 1842; *Cincinnati Gazette*, October 1, 1842. For an indication of the importance of construction in maintaining the local economy in the face of the reduction of specie, see Shaffer, *Directory for 1840,* 483.

14. Cist, *Cincinnati in 1841,* 49; *Niles' National Register,* May 8, 1841; *Proceedings of a Public Meeting of the Citizens of Cincinnati on the Subject of a Western National Armory* (Cincinnati, 1841), 18–19 (cited hereafter as *Western National Armory*).

15. Cist, *Cincinnati in 1841,* 236; *Western National Armory,* 14–17; Michael Chevalier, *Society, Manners, and Politics* (Claremont, Calif., 1949), 203. For a general discussion of the growth of industry in Cincinnati, see Charles Cist, *Cincinnati in 1851* (Cincinnati, 1851), 169–262; Cincinnati *Commercial*, September 14, 1859; and the Federal Writers' Project, *They Built a City: 150 Years of Industrial Cincinnati* (Cincinnati, 1938).

16. Cist's point here was that the value of property was largely in the land rather than in the buildings constructed on it. He explains that most bought property with the intention of constructing new buildings on it, and the presence of old buildings that had to be torn down decreased the general value of the property. Quotation from Cist, *Cincinnati in 1841,* 263–68; Cincinnati *Gazette*, December 14, 1836.

17. *Western National Armory,* 29.

18. Chevalier, *Society, Manners, and Politics,* 203; *Western National Armory,* 29; Cincinnati *Commercial*, January 3, April 16, 1840.

19. *Western National Armory,* 21.

20. Shaffer, *Directory for 1840,* 482–83.

21. O. Farnsworth, ed., *Cincinnati Directory of 1819* (Cincinnati, 1819), 40–42; Shaffer, *Directory for 1840,* 482.

22. Eliza Steel, *A Summer Journey in the West* (New York, 1841), 244–46; Buckingham, *Eastern and Western States,* 2:393; Dickens, *American Notes,* 195–98.

23. Cist, *Cincinnati in 1841,* 111–22; 256–60; Cincinnati *Chronicle,* September 28, 1838. See also John P. Foote, *The Schools of Cincinnati* (Cincinnati, 1855).

24. Benjamin P. Aydelotte, *American Education* (Cincinnati, 1837), 16.
25. The purpose here is to describe the general thrust of the majority decision rather than to analyze voting behavior in detail. For a good general discussion of local government during the earlier period, see Aaron, "Cincinnati, 1818–1838," 101–45.
26. In 1841 the city council granted an individual the rights to supply gas to residents; in 1852 the city organized a paid professional fire department, and the next year a salaried police force.
27. Cincinnati *Advertiser and Journal,* January 1, 27, 28, 29, 30, 31, February 1, 3, 8, 1840; Cincinnati *Gazette,* January 7, 28, February 4, 8, March 27, April 3, 24, 27, 28, 1840; Cincinnati *Commercial,* March 20, 24, 1840.
28. For a running commentary on these two issues in the 1840 election, see the Cincinnati *Gazette* and *Advertiser and Journal* from January through April. The proposed new charter was printed in the *Gazette,* February 17, 1840; the letter from "An Aged Citizen" in the February 15, 1840 issue.
29. Cincinnati *Gazette,* April 10, 1840; Cincinnati *Republican,* April 7, 1841.
30. National politics has purposely been omitted from this discussion because it concerns issues, personalities, and loyalties that extend beyond the local community. It is relevant, however, to mention here that the Whigs dominated national elections in Cincinnati during this period, achieving a 61.5% majority of the 6,314 votes cast in the 1840 presidential election. The Whig strength in the city reflects the general political consensus in the community and the pervasiveness of a (characteristically Whig) confident, corporate concept of society.
31. The spirit of boosterism is discussed in Daniel Boorstein, *The Americans: The National Experience* (New York, 1965), 124–34, and Charles N. Glaab and A. Theodore Brown, *A History of Urban America* (New York, 1967), 71–81. The idea that a sense of "boundlessness" characterized the Jacksonian Age is drawn from John Higham and developed in his short essay *From Boundlessness to Consolidation: The Transformation of American Culture, 1848–1860* (Ann Arbor, 1969). "Community-ism" is described as an ideology here because it seemed to represent, in an age of more narrowly drawn communication and loyalties, a coherent general system of ideas that, like nationalism in a later period, attempted to define the world and the relationship between individuals and society. The term "community-ism" is borrowed from Boorstein who, despite his claims that America is devoid of any ideology, describes this phenomenon very much in terms of an ideology.
32. Jacob Burnet, *The Annual Address Delivered Before the Cincinnati Astronomical Society* (Cincinnati, 1844), 3.
33. Cincinnati *Chronicle,* August 4, 1838.

34. The primary importance of civic order in the community ideology was demonstrated in 1836, when a group of prominent citizens sanctioned the illegal actions of a mob that destroyed the presses of the *Philanthropist.* The significance of this particular incident is that there was nearly unanimous consensus among the community leaders on this issue, and that they decided, at least temporarily, that social order was more important than individual freedom. According to one contemporary authority, Charles Anderson, "every man of influence or property in Cincinnati, save one alone [William A. Corry], was directly or indirectly a party to this outrage upon free speech, free thought, and free press." Henry A. Ford and Kate B. Ford, *History of Cincinnati* (Cincinnati, 1881), 87. Otto Juettner, *Daniel Drake and His Followers* (Cincinnati, 1909), 54.

Chapter 2

1. In fact, the 1840 census figure did not double the 1830 population, but Cist argued that some Cincinnatians were now living outside the corporation limits of the city, in the nearby townships, and that if their number were included, the actual population figure would reach 60,000. Cist, *Cincinnati in 1841,* 35. The Cist figure for the Cincinnati population, 46,382, and the official census figure, 46,338, differ slightly: since Cist was the census taker, I have decided to use his figure. But, in comparing the Cincinnati population composition to that of other cities, I use the figures drawn from the printed census report, *Compendium of the Sixth Census* (Washington, 1841), 76–79.

2. Cist, preface to *Cincinnati in 1851;* and *Cincinnati in 1841,* preface and 233–36.

3. The best short biography of Cist is in the *Dictionary of American Biography.* Frank Cist describes the $100,000 escapade in a typescript summary of Cist's life, sent to the author on January 27, 1967, and deposited with the Cincinnati Historical Society: "Charles Cist had been entrusted with the carriage of a million dollars in currency from St. Louis and Cincinnati to Philadelphia. Arriving too late to deliver [it] to the bank, he put the money in a safe belonging to a man named McAlester. Next morning, a packet containing $100,000 was found missing and Cist, among others, came under suspicion. . . . [T]his packet had evidently slipped through a crack in the back of the safe and had been found intact by a clerk." The president of the Commercial Bank of Cincinnati, among others, published letters in local newspapers that cleared Cist.

4. The impression that Cist became disillusioned with the city's development during the 1850s is based on the change in the general tone and

character of his newspaper articles in the last few years and the last edition of his guidebook, *Cincinnati in 1859* (Cincinnati, 1859). Significantly, this volume looked more to the past than the future, with an extensive section on "early annals" but no essay on the city's "progress and prospects," as there had been in 1841 and 1851.

5. Walker, *Annual Discourse,* 13.

6. W. H. Venable, *Beginnings of Literary Culture in the Ohio Valley* (Cincinnati, 1891), 319.

7. Cist, *Cincinnati in 1841,* 38–39.

8. Perkins, *Memoir and Writings,* 2:245; *Cincinnati Commercial and Literary Gazette,* January 31, 1835.

9. *Transactions of the Fifth Annual Meeting of the Western Literary Institute and College of Professional Teachers* (Cincinnati, 1836), 80.

10. The estimated population of Cincinnati, which suggests the annual rate of increase, is:

1830	24,831	1841	51,010
1831	26,071	1842	55,112
1832	28,014	1843	61,034
1833	27,645	1844	67,907
1834	—	1845	74,699
1835	29,000	1846	82,167
1836	—	1847	90,384
1837	—	1848	99,422
1838	—	1849	109,314
1839	42,500	1850	115,438
1840	46,381		

From Cist, *Cincinnati in 1841,* 38; Ford and Ford, *History of Cincinnati,* 90; and *Annual Reports of . . . the City of Cincinnati* (Cincinnati, 1901), 850–51.

11. As will be demonstrated later, these figures are not really an accurate indicator of growth, since they include different groups within the total population.

12. This argument assumes that the annual influx of newcomers in a city is considerably greater than that indicated by the aggregate increase in population over a decade, because many people stay for only a short period of time. Thus, while the Cincinnati population increased from 1830 to 1840 by almost 25,000, it is possible that a much larger number of people—perhaps two, three, or even four times that number—passed through the city during that decade. This important point about urban population turnover is described in considerable detail in Peter Knights, *The Plain People of Boston* (New York, 1971). Walker, "Notes from Ohio,"

New England Magazine I (1831): 30; Charles Cist, *The Cincinnati Directory for 1843* (Cincinnati, 1843), 3.

13. This analysis of *priority* is similar in method but different in its results than the more common method of determining *persistence* in order to study mobility. Priority traces backward while persistence traces forward: if the size of the population remained constant, the rates would be the same. However, if the population was growing, as it was in Cincinnati, the rate of priority would be higher than that of persistence, since the base population—the last rather than the first year of the trace period—would be larger. The persistence rate for a sample drawn from the 1831 *Directory* and traced to the *Directory for 1840* was 24.8%.

14. Lewis A. Leonard, *Life of Alphonso Taft* (New York, 1920), 38–41; Ford and Ford, *History of Cincinnati*, 136; "The Cincinnati Sojourn of Augustus Roundy, 1838–1845," *Historical and Philosophical Society of Ohio* 19 (1961): 253–64.

15. For biographies of Nast and Reemlin, see Ford and Ford, *History of Cincinnati*, 128–29, 130–31; for Ball, see Maurice Joblin, *Cincinnati Past and Present* (Cincinnati, 1872), 150–54.

16. For Chase and Burnet, see the *Dictionary of American Biography;* for the others, see *Cincinnati Past and Present*, 39, 93, 423, and 431.

17. Aaron, "Cincinnati 1818–1838," particularly the appendix, is an excellent description of this group and the development of their sense of identity.

18. Cist, *Cincinnati in 1841*, 38–39.

19. Edith Perkins Cunningham, *Owl's Nest: A Tribute to Sara Elliott Perkins* (n.p., 1907), 68.

20. "An Eastern Doctor Visits Cincinnati," edited by Phillip Jordan, *Ohio State Medical Journal* 41 (1945): 1120; Alfred G. W. Carter, *The Old Court-House* (Cincinnati, 1880), 120.

21. An analysis of the nativity of the men listed in Venable as being members of the Buckeye Club and Semi-Colon Club reflects the general difference in composition, although there were some New Englanders in the former and non-New Englanders in the latter, as well as some in both. Daniel Drake, born in Kentucky, described himself as a Buckeye, saying "Buckeyeism belongs to the *country,* a better soil for rearing Buckeyes than the town," and that he, like most Buckeyes, became so "by engrafting, or rather by inoculation." Venable, *Beginnings of Literary Culture,* 318.

22. Bernard E. McClellan, "Cincinnati's Response to Abolitionism, 1835–1845" (master's thesis, University of Cincinnati, 1963), 65–73.

23. Ford and Ford, *History of Cincinnati,* 127–46.

24. Ibid., 91, 129, 138–39.

25. Charles Dickens, *American Notes* (Boston, 1842), 199; *The Christian Examiner* 67 (March 1851), 159.

26. The proportion of white men between the ages of twenty and fifty within the total adult white male population of the five largest cities in 1840 was New York (24.2%), Philadelphia (21.1%), Baltimore (21.2%), Boston (30.8%), and New Orleans (35.6%). This may be a good measure of the proportion of newcomers, since they seem to be predominantly young men.

27. Cincinnati *Gazette*, August 21, 1840.

28. Ibid.

29. The following analysis is based on a computerized data bank of the 1840 manuscript census. Since the names were often illegible, they were not included. But every household was included, with the number of members in each age and sex and occupational category recorded. The data in the 1840 census provides aggregate information on household composition within broad general categories—i.e., men between the ages of twenty and thirty, females from five to ten years old, professionals, etc.— which makes direct positive family size and composition analysis fairly impossible. The following attempt is based on certain distinctive groupings that seem to represent different family types.

30. A closer examination of these family-type groupings will be included in a general discussion of Cincinnati demography to be published separately.

31. Unfortunately, the particular character of these large census families is usually not clear. Some can be determined from the name of the family head, but in most cases the names are illegible.

32. This large proportion of boarders within the Cincinnati population may well be unique.

33. Unfortunately, the 1840 census does not indicate the ages of the heads of the census families directly. In most cases, however, it was obvious because there was only one male adult enumerated in the age categories; in the 1,556 families where there was more than one male adult present, the age of the oldest man was arbitrarily taken as the age of the family head, unless there was no female of comparable age, and there were a couple of younger adults, and children, in which case the younger man was assumed to be the family head. According to this somewhat imprecise method, only 2,184 (29.7%) of the 7,364 male family heads were in their twenties; the remaining 5,137 men in their twenties who were not heads of census families represent 71.2% of the total 7,321 men in their twenties and 80.1% of the total 6,431 boarders. In the large census families with more than 12 members, there were 3,522 men, 594 women, and 1,448 children under twenty years of age. Finally, in the 2,658 census families with fewer than

13 members, but more than a pair of adults, only 821 had both extra males and females, who might have been married. Cist, *Cincinnati in 1841.*

34. Ibid., 33.

35. Peter Knights, *Plain People,* includes several appendixes discussing these two sources. His general point is that the census is a better source than city directories because determining the usefulness of these sources is not so much a question of "completeness"—which assumes both were attempting to include the same population—as the particular definition of that population. Both sources may be equally complete but include very different populations, enumerated by very different criteria.

36. Cist, *Cincinnati in 1851,* iv.

37. Larry Gara, "A Correspondent's View of Cincinnati in 1839," *Quarterly Bulletin of the Historical and Philosophical Society of Ohio* 9 (1951): 139–40.

38. Cist, *Cincinnati in 1841,* 235.

39. Between 1830 and 1860 Cincinnati's population increased 549%, greater than any of the ten major cities. Knights, *Plain People,* 21.

40. *Cincinnati Journal* 7 (1834): 130.

41. C. D. Arfwedson, *The United States and Canada, in 1832, 1833, and 1834* (London, 1834), 132–33; Buckingham, *Eastern and Western States,* 2:413–14.

42. Cincinnati *Republican,* December 31, 1840.

43. Cincinnati *Gazette,* January 18, 1842; Cincinnati *Commercial,* January 25, 1843.

44. In 1839, by comparison, there were only 120 paupers in the city according to James Perkins, *Memoir and Writings,* 1:116; official figures were available only starting in 1841 in the Cincinnati *Gazette,* January 27, 1845. See William A. Baughin, "Nativism in Cincinnati before 1860," (master's thesis, University of Cincinnati, 1963), 44–96, for a good description of the pattern of anti-German sentiment during the 1840s.

45. Cincinnati *Enquirer,* October 10, 1844; Cincinnati *Weekly Messenger,* February 27, 1843.

46. Ford and Ford, *History of Cincinnati,* 92. *The Philanthropist,* September 8 to October 6, 1841, carried a complete report of this riot and the results, with reprints of articles form the local newspapers, to show this unjustified pattern of equal blame.

47. Baughin, "Nativism," 59–60; Cincinnati *Commercial,* August 9, 1842; Cincinnati *Gazette,* August 12, 1842.

48. Greve, *Centennial History of Cincinnati,* 614; Cincinnati *Republican,* January 13, 1842; Cincinnati *Gazette,* January 13, 1842; Cincinnati *Commercial,* January 14, 1842.

49. Zinn, "Diary," 156–57, 214, Cincinnati Historical Society.

50. Ibid., 83; Cincinnati *Commercial,* January 4, 1842.
51. Margaret Rives King, *A Memento of Ancestors and Ancestral Homes* (Cincinnati, 1890), 98.
52. *Chronicle,* March 16, 1842.

Chapter 3

1. Perkins, *Memoir and Writings,* 1:1–106.
2. Ibid., 114–18.
3. Ibid., 499–508.
4. Ibid., 116. E. Peabody's laudatory review of Perkins's *Memoir and Writings* includes some valuable personal insights concerning Perkins's character and Cincinnati society: *The Christian Examiner and Religious Miscellany* 50 (March 1851): 157–74.
5. Perkins, *Memoir and Writings,* 1:60.
6. Charles Fenno Hoffman, *A Winter in the West* (New York, 1835), 110; *Christian Examiner* 67 (March 1851): 159; Cincinnati *Commercial,* June 25, 1853, January 1, 1840.
7. *Mirror and Chronicle* 4 (1835): 387; *Philanthropist,* July 22, 1836.
8. Perkins, *Memoir and Writings,* 2:425; Walker, *Annual Discourse,* 26.
9. [Alonzo Garcelon], "A Correspondent's View of Cincinnati in 1839," *Historical and Philosophical Society of Ohio* (1951): 135; Thomas Low Nichols, *Forty Years of American Life* (New York, 1969), 150–51; James Hall, *Statistics of the West,* 24–25; *Western National Armory,* 8.
10. Numerous biographies of Longworth recount the story of his property acquisition, but the best source is his own description of his career, delivered in a speech and published in the Cincinnati *Commercial,* February 25, 1859. Charles Cist gives an interesting picture of the man in *Cincinnati in 1851,* 333–38.
11. The original property tax list for Cincinnati in 1838 is in the Ohio Historical Society. Real estate in Cincinnati in 1838 was assessed at $4,935,500, personal estate at $1,574,516. The assessed value of real estate did not increase significantly from 1835 to 1838 and had only doubled since 1827, despite the great growth of the city. *Annual Reports of the City of Cincinnati* (Cincinnati, 1868).
12. Cist, *Cincinnati in 1851,* 73.
13. This analysis is based on a computerized analysis of the manuscript Tax Records for Hamilton County (Cincinnati) for 1838 in the Ohio State Historical Society. This was the last year for which these records were available, which explains why the 1840 records were not used here. But there is no reason to believe that the general pattern of property ownership

changed much during these two years, or that the delayed local recession from the 1837 depression would have affected a significant number of estates differently in 1840 than in 1838. This impression is confirmed by a newspaper article on the 3,612 property holders in Cincinnati in 1844. It shows that:

1 man held property worth at least					$500,000.
6 men "	"	"	'	"	$200,000.
26 men "	"	"	'	"	$100,000.
43 men "	"	"	'	"	$50,000.
56 men "	"	"	'	"	$30,000.
73 men "	"	"	'	"	$20,000.
82 men "	"	"	'	"	$15,000.
118 men "	"	"	'	"	$10,000.
423 men "	"	"	'	"	$5,000.
645 men "	"	"	'	"	$2,000.
826 men "	"	"	'	"	$1,000.
1,313 men "	"	"	'	"	$100.

Cincinnati Business Directory for 1844 (Cincinnati, 1844), vi.

14. Of the 643 men not positively identified in the *Directory for 1840,* 293 had names that could not be traced, or had several comparable, but not identical, history listings that were not matched. Of the rest, some were probably absentee owners, some were children, and some moved from the city between 1838 and 1839. The possibility that many of these property owners with no directory listing were, in fact, German or transient boarders has been dismissed because of the relative youthfulness and rootlessness of these groups, and the small proportion of Germans (4%), rivermen (1%), and boarders (4%) who were property owners included in the directory.

The decile distribution of these 863 property owners who were identified in the directory was: 10.2%, 10.1%, 9.8%, 10.1%, 10.0%, 10.0%, 9.7%, 10.4%, 9.7%, 10.0%.

15. An analysis of five different tax lists and the 1860 census indicates that the number of property owners within the total population (including children) dropped from 24% in 1799, to 10% in 1805, to 7% in 1817, to 6% in 1838, to 5.5% in 1855, and 6.5% in the 1860 census (counting only heads of families owning real property). During this period, in 1839 only 16% of the directory males had been in the 1831 directory, in 1850 only 18% of the directory males had been in the 1840 directory, and in 1860 only 15% of the directory males had been in the 1850 directory.

16. Cincinnati *Gazette,* August 4, 1840.

17. Perkins, *Memoir and Writings*, 1:119; *Compendium of the Sixth Census*, 79; Buckingham, *Eastern and Western States*, 2:390.
18. *The Christian Examiner*, 67 (1851): 14; Cist, *Cincinnati in 1841*, 42–43. The percentage of the population which was employed in New York (20.5%), Baltimore (12.1%), New Orleans (15.1%), Philadelphia (17.7%), Boston (20.3%), Brooklyn (26.3%), Albany (6.5%), Charleston (8.2%), Washington (5.0%), and the total national population (28.1%) was computed from the *Compendium of the Sixth Census*.
19. Cincinnati *Commercial and Literary Gazette*, February 23, 1833.
20. "Sojourn of Augustus Roundy," 261; Chambrun, *Making of Longworth*, 63. For a good description of the experiences of professionals, particularly lawyers, and the difficulties they had in getting a start, see the Peter Zinn Diary, Cincinnati Historical Society; and James Wickes Taylor, *A Choice Nook of Memory: The Diary of a Cincinnati Clerk, 1842–1844*, edited by James Taylor Dunn (Columbus, 1950). For the careers of Cincinnati's more successful lawyers during this period, see Alfred G. W. Carter, *The Old Court House* (Cincinnati, 1880); Robert B. Warden, *The Private Life and Public Services of Salmon Portland Chase* (Cincinnati, 1874), 182–231; Lewis A. Leonard, *Life of Alphonso Taft* (New York, 1920), 35–45; and for conditions by midcentury, *The Diary and Letters of Rutherford B. Hayes*, vol. 1, edited by Charles R. Williams (Columbus, 1922).
21. The primacy of Cincinnati merchants in local life during the first fifty years of the city's life is indicated in Richard Wade, *The Urban Frontier* (Cambridge, 1959), 105–8; and documented more fully in Aaron, "Cincinnati, 1818–1838."
22. James Hall, *Statistics of the West*, 1–2; Cincinnati *Advertiser and Journal*, July 9, 1840.
23. The distinction between the merchants and shopkeepers is evident in Shaffer's *Directory for 1840*, which identifies the former group by the name of establishment (i.e., "John D. Jones [J. J. & D. L. Co.]") and the latter by trade (i. e., "William Jones, Grocer").
24. Cist, *Cincinnati in 1841*, 54–58. The *Directory for 1840*, however, does not distinguish the particular occupation and will be used in the following analysis.
25. *Cincinnati Past and Present*, 101, 31.
26. Discussion of the differences and divisions within this total group of working mechanics—constituting approximately 60% of the Cincinnati working force in 1840—is imprecise and difficult. The most obvious divisions, master mechanic, journeyman, apprentice, and unskilled laborer, were not recorded in the city directories or census; information on the character of the products and the number of workers involved is available

in the aggregate, but does not indicate the variety of worker specialization and status within that particular industry. Dictionaries of occupations for the late nineteenth and twentieth centuries are unsatisfactory, since the nature and status of many jobs changed greatly over the period.

27. Cincinnati *Commercial,* January 3, 1853; April 15, 1852.

28. *The Cincinnati Business Directory for 1844* (Cincinnati, 1844), VI; Cincinnati *Commercial,* December 27, 1855; October 6, 1857; undated for 1865; James Parton, "Cincinnati," *Atlantic Monthly* 20 (1867): 232.

29. Cincinnati *Commercial,* April 24, 1845; January 1, September 28, 1846; May 4, 1850; June 25, July 2, 1853; May 11, 1852; Eliza Porter, *A Hairdresser's Experience in High Society* (Cincinnati, 1860), 196.

30. Cincinnati *Chronicle,* September 21, 1841.

31. For a good discussion of the General Trades Union, see Aaron, "Cincinnati, 1818–1838," 91–98; Cincinnati *Advertiser and Journal,* February 17, 1840; Cincinnati *Chronicle,* January 14, 1842.

32. Cincinnati *Commercial,* July 30, 1851; March 5, 1852; November 13, 1852; March 22, 1853; March 31, 1854; May 27, 1854.

33. *Cist's Weekly Advertiser,* April 3, 1850; Cincinnati *Gazette,* April 2, 1851; Cincinnati *Commercial,* October 10, 1849; April 16, 1850; August 7, September 26, 1851.

34. Edward D. Mansfield, *Personal Memories: Social, Political, and Literary* (Cincinnati, 1887), 200–201.

35. Cist, *Cincinnati in 1841,* 260–62.

36. Cist, *Miscellany,* 1:162; *Cist's Weekly Advertiser,* July 27, 1847.

37. Although Cist said he based his conclusions on the careers of over 400 merchants, these 37 examples were the only evidence he cited in the article. *Cist's Weekly Advertiser,* July 27, 1847.

38. Ibid., November 5, 1852.

39. Cincinnati *Commercial,* June 21, 1850; April 20, 1849.

40. Cincinnati *Chronicle,* November 16, 1841.

Chapter 4

1. Charles Cist, *Cincinnati in 1851* (Cincinnati, 1851), 341–46, is a good contemporary account of the building of the observatory, written, in part, by Ormsby Mitchel. The records of the Cincinnati Astronomical Society, available on microfilm at the Cincinnati Historical Society, detail its formal activities. Stephen Goldfarb, "Science and Democracy: A History of the Cincinnati Observatory, 1842–1872," *Ohio History* 79, no. 3 (Summer 1969): 172–79, is a good recent review of its early history. Russell McCormmich, "Ormsby MacKnight Mitchel's Sidereal Messenger, 1846–

1848," *Proceedings of the American Philosophical Society* 110, no. 1 (February 1966): 35–47, contains some pertinent biographical information on Mitchel.

2. Cist, *Cincinnati in 1851,* 341.

3. Ibid., 341–44; Goldfarb, "Science and Democracy," 36; McCormmich, "Ormsby Mitchel's Sidereal Messenger," 173–74.

4. Cist, *Cincinnati in 1851,* 341–46; Ormsby M. Mitchel, preface to *The Planetary and Stellar Worlds: A Popular Exposition of the Great Discoveries and Theories of Modern Astronomy—in a Series of Ten Lectures* (New York, 1848), reprinted in the *Bulletin of the Cincinnati Historical Society* 24, no. 2 (April 1966), 164–74; Edward D. Mansfield, *Personal Memories,* 310.

5. Cist, *Cincinnati in 1851,* 341–44; Goldfarb, "Science and Democracy," 172–75: McCormmich, "Ormsby Mitchel's Sidereal Messenger," 35–36.

6. Cist, *Cincinnati in 1851,* 341–46. E. D. Mansfield, a close friend and former law partner of Mitchel's, also described the building of the observatory in somewhat contradictory terms. At one point he said it was "solely the creation" of Mitchel; later he wrote, "The whole work, of which Mitchel was the director and originator, was probably the first and *only* purely scientific enterprise literally carried out by the people." Mansfield, *Personal Memories,* 309–10.

7. In the following discussion I use the term *association* to designate any group, formal or informal, permanent or ephemeral, open or restricted, which was organized for the common benefit of its members and in which participation was voluntary. In general this definition corresponds with that of Tocqueville, in his classic discussion of voluntary associations, in *Democracy in America,* edited by Phillip Bradley (New York, 1945) 2:106–20. As of the 1970s, very little work had been done on associational activity in America during the nineteenth century other than the general essay by Oscar Handlin in *Dimensions of Liberty* (Cambridge, 1961), and Merle Curti's admirable analysis in *The Making of an American Community: A Case Study of Democracy in a Frontier County* (Stanford, 1959), chapters 12, 13, and 15.

8. Perkins, "Associations: A Vital Form of Social Action," in *Memoir and Writings,* 1:165–72. Perkins's discussion, as well as that of Timothy Walker described below, closely parallel Tocqueville's classic analysis of associations in *Democracy in America.* Perkins's essay was first published in 1838, just after the publication of Tocqueville's first volume; Walker's journal (see below, n. 9) was written during the 1830s. There is no internal evidence that either man based his ideas on Tocqueville's analysis, and it may well be that the Frenchman got his inspiration from Americans like Walker and Perkins.

9. Walker, Manuscript Journal, in the Walker Papers, Cincinnati Historical Society.

10. See *History of the Cincinnati Fire Department* (Cincinnati, 1895) for a detailed discussion of these developments.

11. *A History of the Nova Cesarea Harmony Lodge* (Cincinnati, 1928).

12. Cist, *Cincinnati in 1841*, 133–36. For a good description of the activities of the society, particularly the seminars, see the Diary of William Stanley Merrell, 1840, in the Cincinnati Historical Society.

13. Mansfield, *Personal Memories,* 320–22.

14. It is noteworthy that of the 177 activists for whom age information is available, the age distribution is considerably older than that of the 13,705 adult white males:

Ages	Activists (%)	Total Men (%)
20s	7.9	53.4
30s	23.7	27.7
40s	30.5	10.9
50s	27.7	4.9
60s and up	10.2	3.0

15. Walker, Manuscript Journal.

16. Minutes of the Cincinnati Chamber of Commerce, Cincinnati Historical Society.

17. John D. Jones, diary, vol. 1, 65–66. Jones Papers, Cincinnati Historical Society.

18. For Buchanan's "Sketch of a Busy Life," as well as his obituaries, see the Wright Obituaries, Cincinnati Historical Society. The Buchanan Papers, Cincinnati Historical Society, include a number of letters to and from Buchanan written during this period which implicitly suggest this tone of authority and respect in the correspondence.

19. For Langdon's life, see the Langdon Papers, Cincinnati Historical Society. His efforts to hold the assistant postmastership are detailed in letters from E. P. Langdon to R. C. Langdon, January 27, 1841, and E. P. Langdon to Judge McLean, February 5, 1841.

20. Alfred G. W. Carter, *The Old Court House: Reminiscences and Anecdotes of the Courts and Bar of Cincinnati* (Cincinnati, 1880), 73–76.

21. Ibid.

22. Ibid.

23. Greve, *History of Cincinnati,* 659; Kathleen J. Kiefer, "A History of the Cincinnati Fire Department in the Nineteenth Century" (master's thesis, University of Cincinnati, 1967), 46–80, is a good review of these critical years.

24. Ford and Ford, *History of Cincinnati,* 100; Cincinnati *Enquirer,* July 6, 1850.

Afterword

1. A few of the most important studies that complement and fill out Glazer's account are Steven J. Ross, *Workers on the Edge: Work, Politics and Leisure in Industrializing Cincinnati, 1788–1890* (New York, 1985); Henry Louis Taylor Jr., ed., *Race and the City: Work, Community, and Protest in Cincinnati, 1820–1970* (Urbana, 1992); Kathryn Kish Sklar, *Catharine Beecher: A Study in American Domesticity* (New York, 1976); Henry D. Shapiro and Jonathan D. Sarna, eds., *Ethnic Diversity and Civic Identity: Patterns of Conflict and Cohesion in Cincinnati since 1820;* (Urbana, 1992); Jed Dannenbaum, *Drink and Disorder: Temperance Reform in Cincinnati from the Washingtonian Revival to the WCTU* (Urbana, 1984); M. Christine Anderson, "Catholic Nuns and the Invention of Social Work: The Sisters of the Santa Maria Institute of Cincinnati," *Journal of Women's History* (forthcoming, Spring 2000).

2. Arthur Schlesinger, *The Rise of the City* (New York, 1933; Columbus Ohio, 1999); Richard Wade, *The Urban Frontier* (Chicago, 1996; reprint of 1959 edition); Frederick Jackson Turner, *The Frontier in American History* (New York, 1920).

3. For a discussion of "power elite" and "interlocking directorates," see C. Wright Mills, *The Power Elite* (New York, 1956). On pluralism, a good place to start is Robert A. Dahl, *Pluralist Democracy in the United States, Conflict and Consensus* (Chicago, 1967).

4. The literature on republicanism and liberalism in American thought is voluminous. For a useful introduction to the debate and its implications beyond the academy, see Christopher Lasch, *The True and Only Heaven: Progress and Its Critics* (New York, 1991), chap. 5. On the centrality of the Jacksonian city in American historiography, see Sean Wilentz, *Chants Democratic: New York City and the Rise of the American Working Class, 1788–1850* (New York, 1984), especially 6–11; and Ross, *Workers on the Edge,* especially xv–xx.

5. For a brief discussion of modernization theory and Jacksonian America, see Sean Wilentz, "On Class and Politics in Jacksonian America," *Reviews in American History* 10 (December 1982): 52. For the relationship between

modernization theory of the transition from "community" to "society," see Lasch, *The True and Only Heaven,* chap. 4.

6. Ross, *Workers on the Edge,* examines Cincinnati's community ideology with reference to civic republicanism. For a discussion of the role of civic cooperation in Cincinnati's early growth and the rise of social tensions that undercut cooperation, see Carl Abbott, *Boosters and Businessmen* (Westport, Conn., 1981). For the tendency to define the lower orders as the major problem facing the city, see Alan I Marcus, *A Plague of Strangers: Social Groups and the Origins of City Services in Cincinnati, 1819–1870* (Columbus, 1991). A fuller development of the argument sketched here is John D. Fairfield, "Democracy in Cincinnati: Civic Virtue and Three Generations of Urban Historians." *Urban History* 24 (1997): 200–220.

7. As Wilentz argues, "Middle class capitalist ideals were validated (and in part forged) in the creation of a professional party system." Wilentz, "On Class and Politics in Jacksonian America," 56. On "disengagement" and "engaged disbelief," see Glenn C. Altschuler and Stuart M. Blumin, "Limits of Political Engagement in Antebellum America: A New Look at the Golden Age of Participatory Democracy," *Journal of American History* 84 (December 1997): 855–85, and the various responses.

Index

URBAN LIFE AND URBAN LANDSCAPE SERIES

Zane L. Miller, General Editor

*The series examines the history of urban life and
the development of the urban landscape through works that
place social, economic, and political issues in the intellectual and
cultural context of their times.*